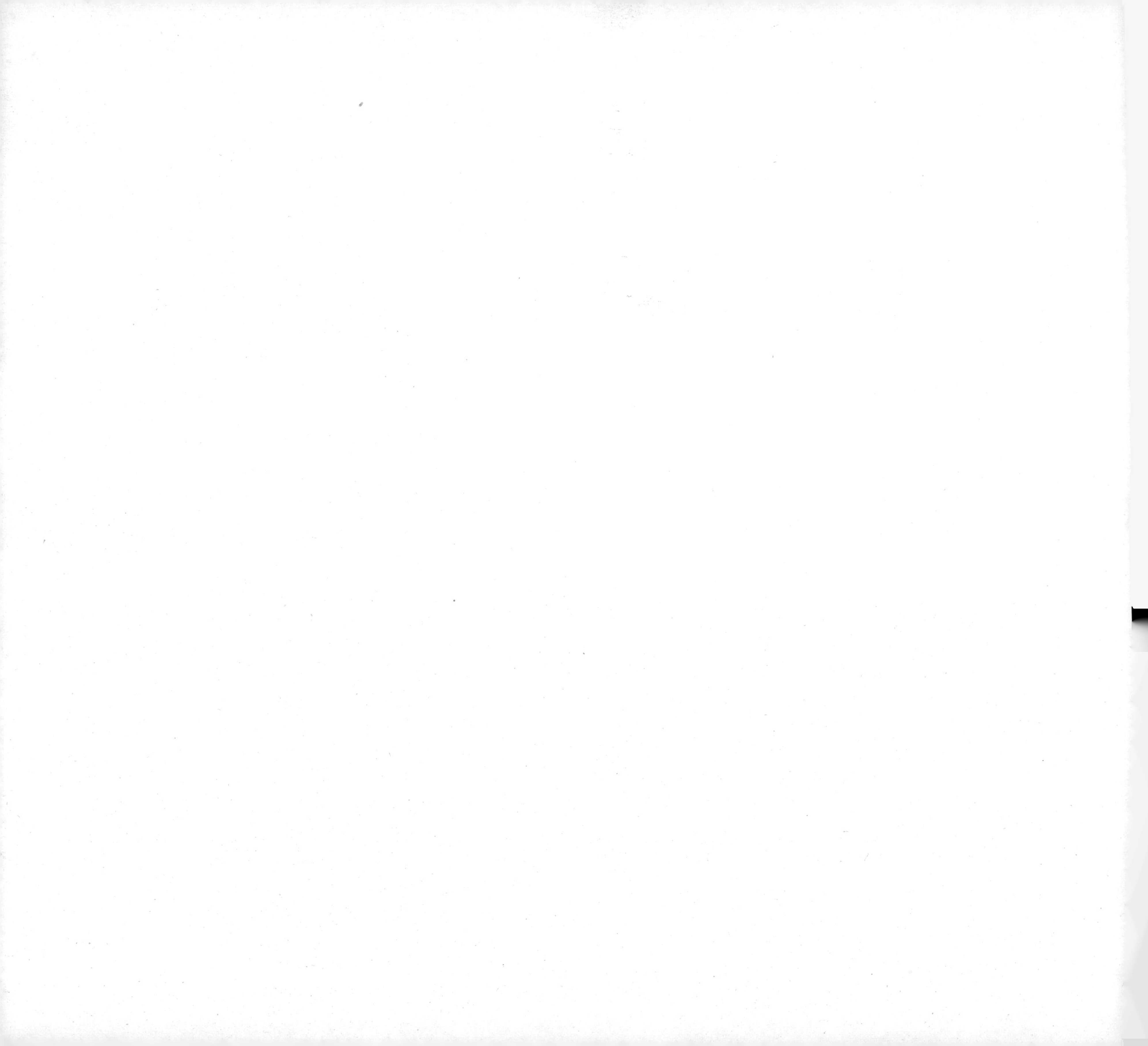

IMAGO MUNDI
XVIII

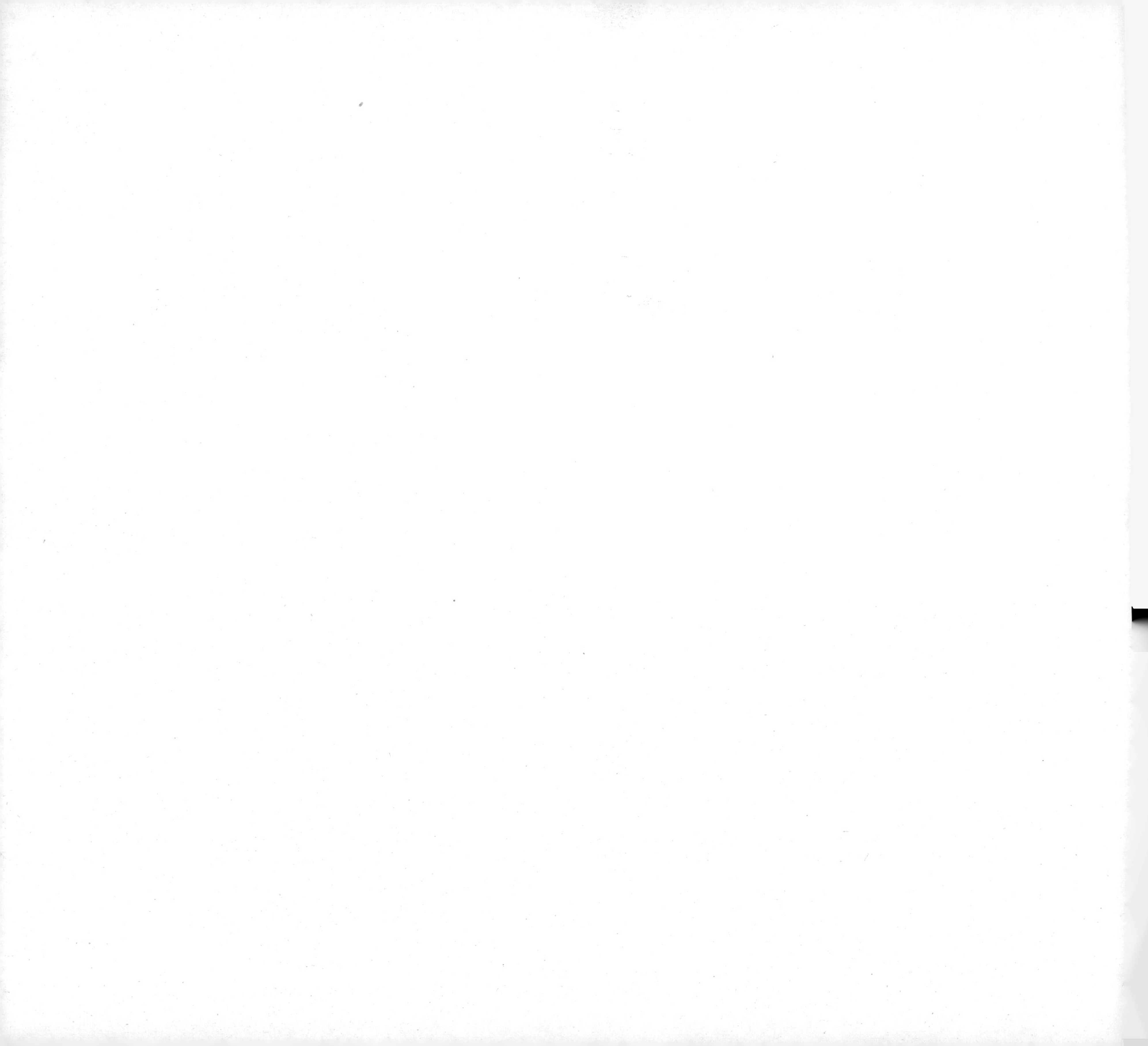

SEBASTIAN SCHUTYSER

Flowers of the Moon

AFROALPINE VEGETATION OF THE RWENZORI MOUNTAINS

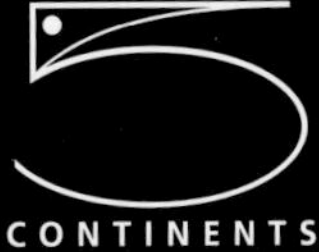

5 CONTINENTS

Photographs and text by Sebastian Schutyser
Drawings by Raf De Martelaere
Cartography by François Gallier

Editorial coordination
Laura Maggioni

Art direction
Lara Gariboldi

Editing
Andrew Ellis

Thanks to:

Alex Gysel
John Kireru, and his team of porters
Olov & Inga Hedberg
Peter Linder
Berit Gehrke
Ulf Amundsen
Raf De Martelaere
Karim Grusenmeyer
Bart Deseyn
François Gallier
Marnix Vermeulen
For their share in the creation of this work.

Belgian Vocation Foundation
The Flemish Government
Rwenzori Mountaineering Services
For their generous support for this work.

Eric Ghysels and his 5 Continents Editions team
*For having the spirit to publish this work, and shaping
my raw materials into this book.*

Colour separation
Eurofotolit, Cernusco sul Naviglio (Milan)

Printed in Italy in July 2007 by
Conti Tipocolor, Calenzano (Florence)

CONTENTS

6 MAP OF THE RWENZORI MOUNTAINS

8 THE AFROALPINE VEGETATION OF THE RWENZORI MOUNTAINS
Sebastian Schutyser

20 BIOGRAPHY

22 CAPTIONS

24 PHOTOGRAPHS

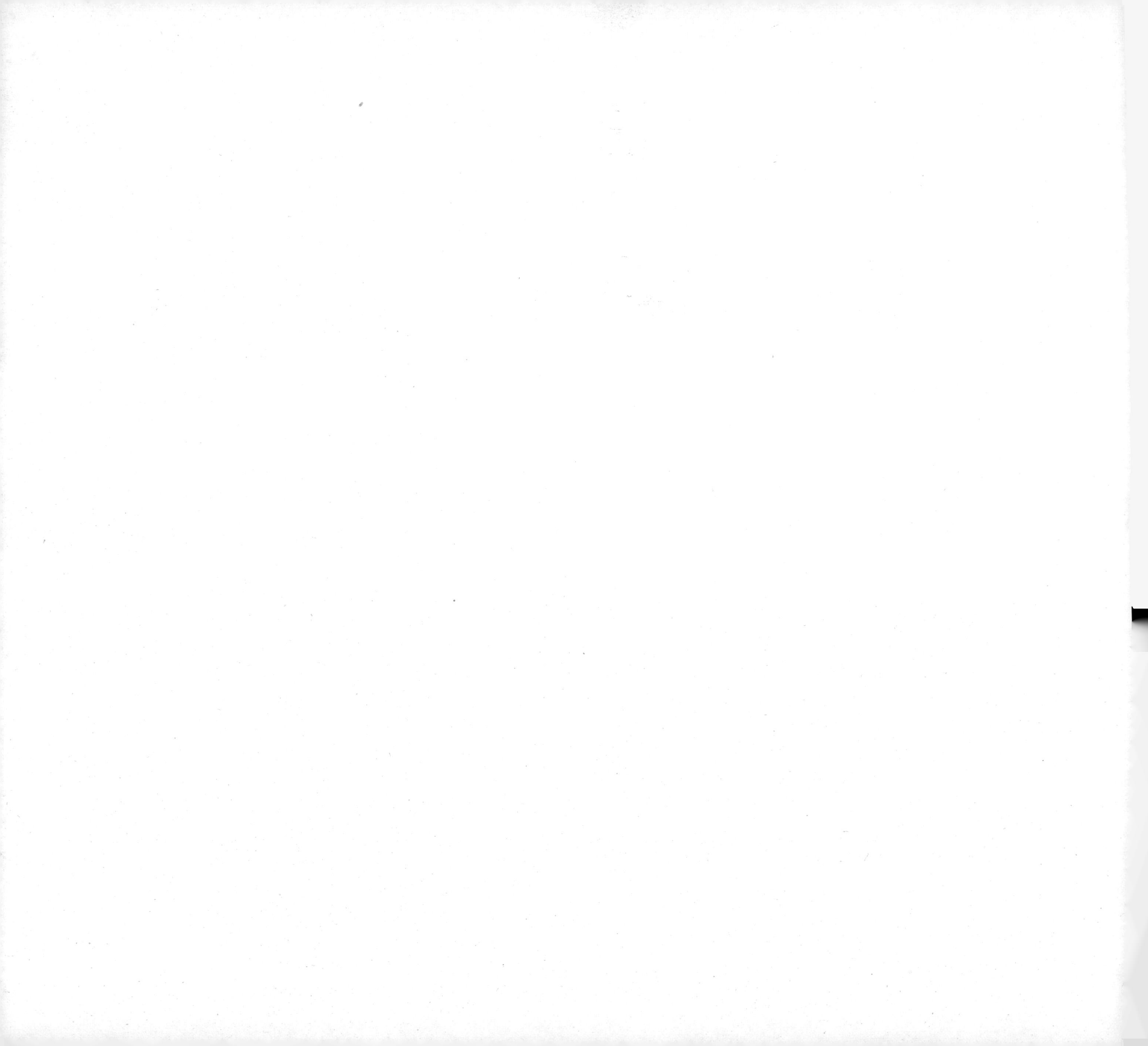

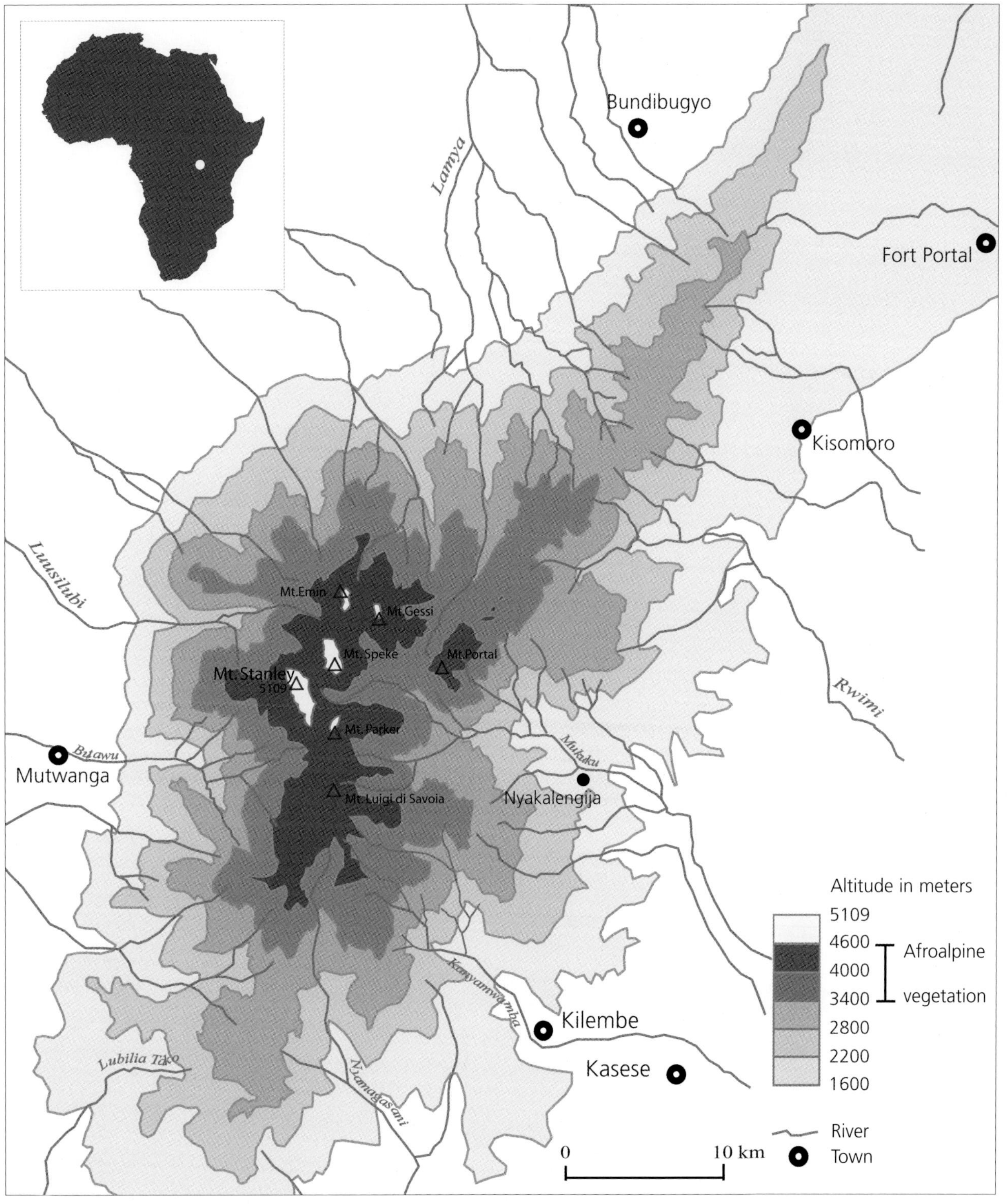

Bundibugyo
Fort Portal
Kisomoro
Lamya
Luusilubi
Mt.Emin
Mt.Gessi
Mt.Speke
Mt.Portal
Mt.Stanley
5109
Mt.Parker
Mt.Luigi di Savoia
Butawu
Mutwanga
Mubuku
Nyakalengija
Rwimi
Kanyamwamba
Kilembe
Kasese
Lubilia Tako
Nyamugasani
Altitude in meters
5109
4600
4000
3400
2800
2200
1600
Afroalpine
vegetation
River
Town
0
10 km

AFROALPINE VEGETATION OF THE RWENZORI MOUNTAINS

Sebastian Schutyser

LUNAE MONTES

In the heart of Africa, on top of the equator, and higher than any other mountain range on this continent, lies a snow-capped massif with a mythical resonance: the Mountains of the Moon. Thus referred to in AD 150 by the Alexandrian Greek Ptolemy, the snows of these Lunae Montes were supposed to be feeding the sources of the Nile. More a bibliographer than an intrepid explorer himself, Ptolemy relied on the claims of an obscure traveller. Today, we know these mountains as the Rwenzori. Oddly enough, a neighbouring region is known by its inhabitants as Wunyamwezi, or Land of the Moon. Could it be that Ptolemy's information was more precise than we may believe, or did he just sample from various reports? Hard to tell, but the name has stuck.

Other ancient Greeks have written on the presumed origins of the Nile in terms which may point to the Rwenzori. In the fifth century AD Aeschylus mentioned "Egypt nurtured by snows", and Herodotus stated that the River Nile sprang from a bottomless lake between two sharp peaks, Crophi and Mophi. One hundred years later Aristotle spoke of a Silver Mountain being the source of the Nile. What ties these and posterior Arab accounts together, is the quest for the sources of the Nile and a fascination for such a wondrous thing as eternal snow in equatorial Africa. Neither did I escape the spell when first learning about it. My first steps in photography were directed by the desire to evoke a different Africa, far from the persistent clichés that determine our conception of the continent. And here a perfect opportunity arose.

These mind-tickling factors, and the sheer inaccessibility of the area, have added an air of mystery to the mists and clouds that cling to it. Although other mountains, among which Africa's highest peak Kilimanjaro, have been claiming the legendary name, the Rwenzori have won the day. They are now widely accepted to be the Mountains of the Moon. After all, aren't they the highest water supplier of the Nile, through Lake Albert? Would it not be fair then to consider them indeed as those "high snows which feed the Nile"? It certainly was my own intuition on a cold, moonlit night at the Irene Lakes, high up in the Rwenzori, when very sudden and silently, snowflakes were all around me.

WHITE PEAKS IN DARKEST AFRICA

Despite all these millenary stories, it took a very long time for the Rwenzori to be discovered. Of course, the indigenous Bakonzo have lived at its foot and hunted there for ages. But they did not venture into the world of snow and ice that dominates the central area. This they considered to be the dwellings of the divine, and off-limits to themselves. The first well-documented sighting was

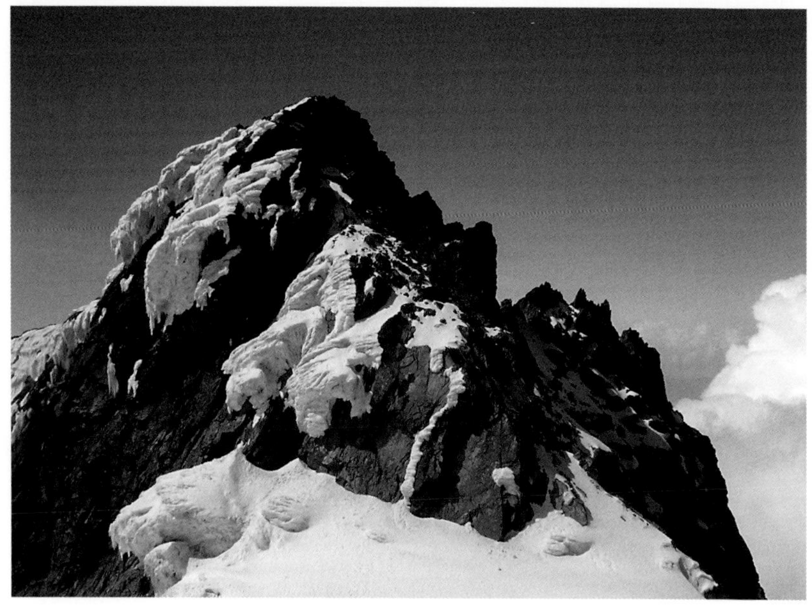

"white" area. Sella recorded this in a series of magnificent images. He combined great technical skill and a true sense of beauty. The depth of his photographs is becoming rare in an age of digital cameras. Apparently it is not only the glaciers that are melting away in our times…

SELLA'S PHOTOGRAPHIC WORK IS CONSERVED AT THE MUSEO NAZIONALE DELLA MONTAGNA, IN TURIN, AND AT THE ISTITUTO DI FOTOGRAFIA ALPINA VITTORIO SELLA, IN BIELLA, BOTH IN ITALY. THE UNIVERSITY OF MAKERERE, UGANDA, ALSO HAS A SELECTION OF HIS IMAGES. A GOOD DEAL OF SELLA'S PHOTOGRAPHS WERE REPUBLISHED IN *THE RUWENZORI DISCOVERY* BY ROBERTO MANTOVANI, AND A SMALLER SELECTION IN DAVID PLUTH'S *UGANDA RWENZORI, A RANGE OF IMAGES*, MAKING THE REMAINING COLOUR PICTURES IN THIS ALBUM LOOK RATHER BLEAK.

officially made by Sir Henry Morton Stanley in 1888. Before that, several Europeans came near enough to spot it, but passed on their way unawares, the elusive peaks being occulted by clouds. Funnily enough, Stanley must have been among them, as the enormous blue mass he distinguished on his earlier transcontinental expedition in 1876, almost undoubtedly was the Rwenzori Range of his *In darkest Africa*.

The next breakthrough in the exploration of the impervious mountains was the Italian mountaineering expedition led by Prince Luigi Amedeo Giuseppe Maria Ferdinando Francesco de Savoia, Duke of the Abruzzi, in 1906. At an amazing speed they made first ascents of all major snow and ice peaks, mapping their complex geography *en passant*, and leaving them with elegant Italian names. Early risers, they took full advantage of the frequently clear weather in the wee hours of the day. Their team consisted of mountain guides, biologists, surveyors, a geologist, photographers, and some one hundred and fifty porters. Photographer Vittorio Sella left us perhaps the most valuable heritage of all: a collection of vintage photographs showing a vanished world. A hundred years ago abundant snow and fiendish ice formations covered nearly a tenfold of the present

Explorers, scientists, and adventurers have since then been adding to the knowledge of this last great mountain discovery of the world, on the border of present Uganda and the Congo. Many of its mysteries have been unravelled. Yet, there is still a Rwenzori unknown. The reason for this lies in the location between the equatorial forests of the Congo and the monsoon climate of eastern Africa, which produces a constant veil of clouds. Added to the scrambled topography and muddy conditions, the abundant rainfall causes a vegetation so rampant that it turns penetration into a real ordeal. And these hardships do not even guarantee the visitor a glimpse of the peaks, which may remain hidden for days on end. Due to its inaccessibility, most parts of the mountains are seldom or never frequented. In fact, this uninhabited, cold and wet universe is the last inviolate chunk of pure nature on the African continent.

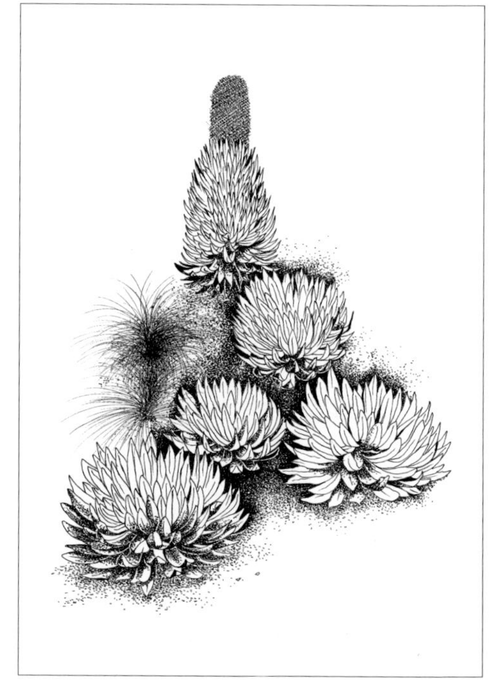

FIG. I
Alexandra Peak,
5,091m

FIG. 2
Lobelia bequaertii

SOME FACTS ABOUT GEOLOGY AND CLIMATE

The Rwenzori mountains form an extremely steep and rugged mountain range approximately 50 kilometres wide and 120 kilometres long. They lie south to Lake Albert, and just north of the equator. In the west, the range is tilted steeply towards the Congo basin, with gentler eastern slopes in Uganda, which includes about 80% of its surface. With more than twenty peaks above 4.500 metres altitude, culminating in the 5.109 metres of Margherita Peak, they tower over the European Alps. They are also the highest mountain range of Africa, only surpassed in height by the isolated extinct volcanic cones of Kilimanjaro and Mount Kenya. Unlike these, the Rwenzori are not volcanic in origin.

They originated about 10 million years ago by an enormous uplift of Pre-Cambrian rocks, during the development of the Great Rift Valley. The combination of violent upthrust and hard rock gives the Rwenzori massif its serrated alpine character. It was subsequently deeply carved by rivers and glaciers. Glacial erosion has sculpted cirques and left many moraines and bogs. Most of the approximately 50 lakes are also of glacial origin. They appear in various kinds and sizes, adding to the beauty and diversity of the landscape. Some of them are quite deep, and have subterranean outlets. Lake Bujuku is one of the most frequented, and is heart-shaped if you look at it from a certain angle. The scenic twin lakes of Kitandara are beckoning the tired mountaineer on his descent from the Scott-Elliot Pass, while the off-the-beaten-track Lac de la Lune (or Moon Lake) makes one feel scared of the void behind its moraine. In stark contrast, the highest central peaks are permanently covered with snowfields and retreating glaciers, while lower peaks still receive annual snowfall. The Rwenzori are a vital water catchment area. The upland bogs act as a huge sponge which absorbs and regulates the precipitation. The range is the highest and most permanent source of the River Nile and supplies water and protection from flooding for the lowland populations.

The Rwenzori trap the humid air of the Congo basin and are very wet indeed. Rain is falling on most days, even in the drier periods. There are two "rainy" seasons, from March to May, and from September to December. During that time a rain-curtain closes over the range almost constantly. Clouds and fog become very persistent. Average annual rainfall is around 2500 millimetres in the higher areas, where it often falls as snow or hail. There are local differences related with the topography. At high elevations temperatures swing daily from above to below freezing, but seasonal variations are minimal. Ice rime forms on mountain ridges as a result of freezing mists. Unfortunately, the huge and wonderful rime cauliflowers which used to adorn the main peaks are vanishing as the glaciers are shrinking.

FOR A BETTER UNDERSTANDING OF THE RWENZORI MOUNTAINS IN ALL THEIR ASPECTS, I STRONGLY RECOMMEND THE RECENTLY REPUBLISHED *GUIDE TO THE RWENZORI* BY HENRY OSMASTON. THIS BOOK IS AN ESSENTIAL PART OF YOUR MOUNTAINEER EQUIPMENT IF YOU ARE HEADING FOR THE PEAKS, AS WELL AS THE *MAP AND GUIDE TO THE RWENZORI* BY ANDREW WIELOCHOWSKI.

FAIRY-TALE FORESTS...

The Rwenzori are well known for their extravagant plants. Although the flora is closely related to that of other east-African high mountains, and similar-looking species occur in the Andes, it is much more luxuriant here. This is mainly a result of the high and regular rainfall in the area. The distribution of vegetation is for a good deal determined by the altitude, but the nature of the site plays an important role as well. A well-sheltered valley may grow species one would expect in lower zones. There are a lot of overlapping areas. Yet distinct altitudinal zones can be observed. At higher elevations, certain genera of plants grow unusually large. Most surprising are the giant heathers, senecios and lobelias. Combined with wild and rugged mountain landscapes, they evoke a primeval atmosphere, which dwarfs the visitor. For one thing, it made me feel as if walking in a real Jurassic Park. Without dinosaurs.

But I am running ahead of things. Let me try to give a brief description of the consecutive altitudinal zones and their vegetation, starting where all visitors do: in the grassy foothills of the mountains. High-growing elephant grass is common here, but most of the foothill region is now cultivated. Above 1,500 metres in altitude, the grasses converge into montane forests. Contrary to tropical forests, trees rarely grow over 30 metres here, and the canopy is well broken. This allows a very tangled undergrowth to develop, which makes the going tough. Remarkable are the giant tree-ferns. Large animal tracks occasionally show. Dinosaurs may be a thing of the past, but elephants are not (yet), and on my second visit I nearly stepped into the physical proof of their presence. Their numbers are few, but it is best to remain cautious. With some luck, one may come across blue monkeys and Rwenzori Colobus monkeys, or hear the screeching of chimpanzee. At 2,500 metres the forest starts to give way to dense concentrations of bamboo, which is actually a form of giant grass. It thrives mostly on the better soils, while the ridge tops are occupied by the first giant heather trees, or *Erica*. On steep slopes, *Mimulopsis elliottii* forms an impenetrable thicket. *Hagenia abyssinica* is a large tree with fernlike leaves. Also appearing on well-watered grounds are the first single-stemmed giant lobelias, *Lobelia gibberoa*. And with them, my first exposures of the extended Afroalpine family.

In the following altitudinal belt, roughly between 3,000 and 4,000 metres, the heather trees are monopolising the poor soils, such as rocky grounds and ridge tops. Up to 10 metres high, they grow in dense concentrations. Their branches are often adorned with Old Man's Beard, or *Usnea* lichen. Emerging from the fog, the bony silhouettes of these giant heathers have a ghostly look, as the wind is softly stirring the grey-greenish threads of lichen. Their roots and the ground are carpeted with a thick growth of mosses, dotted with small ferns. Where the tree stems and branches are strong enough to support the weight, the heathers are also swaddled by undulating moss cushions. When mists dissolve, and sunrays are raking through this gnarled labyrinth, the gloom is lifted and the mosses burst into vivid greens, deep bronzes, and saturated reddish-browns. Underneath there is an inextricable jumble of dead wood, only slowly decomposing due to the cold and the acid conditions. The

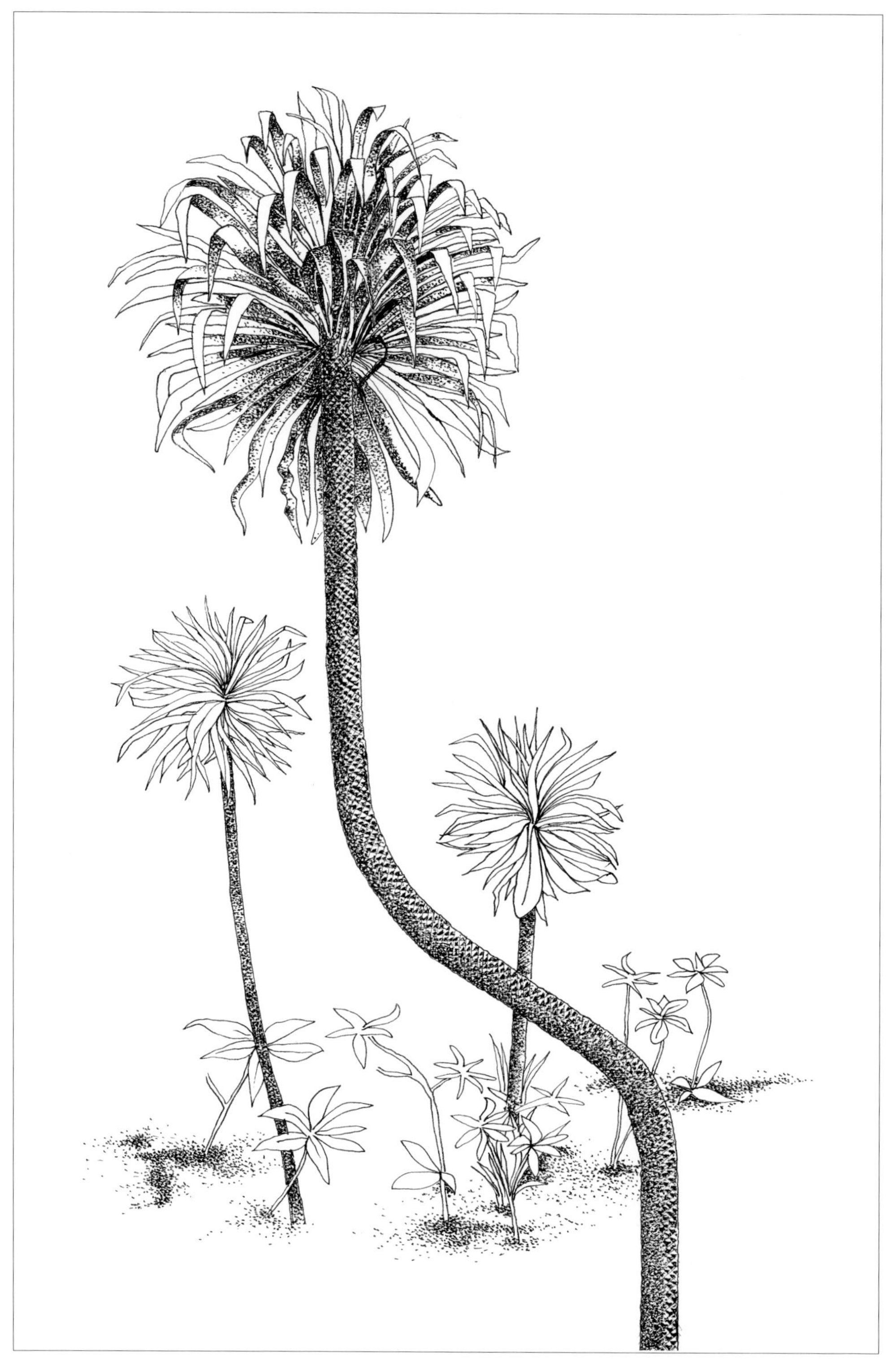

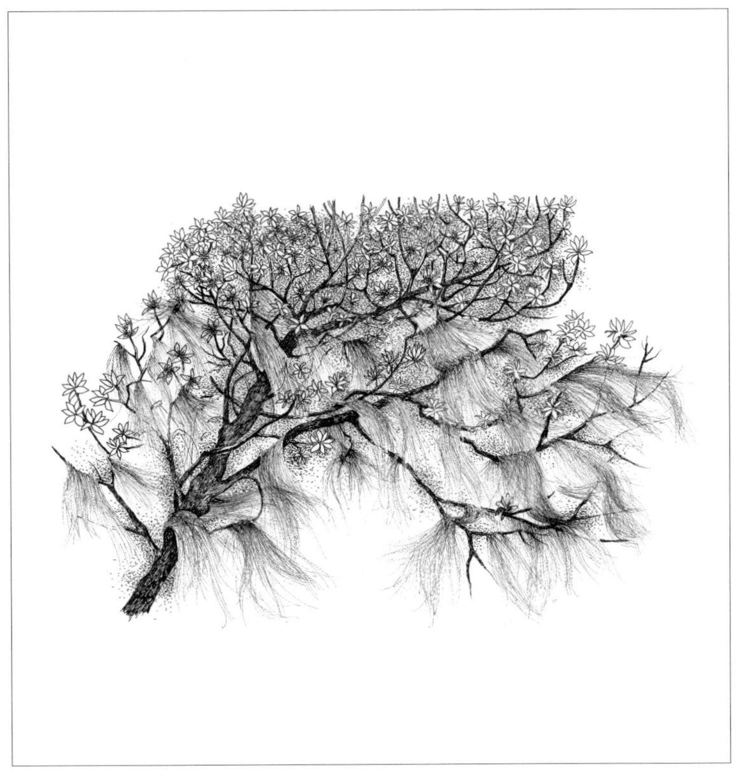

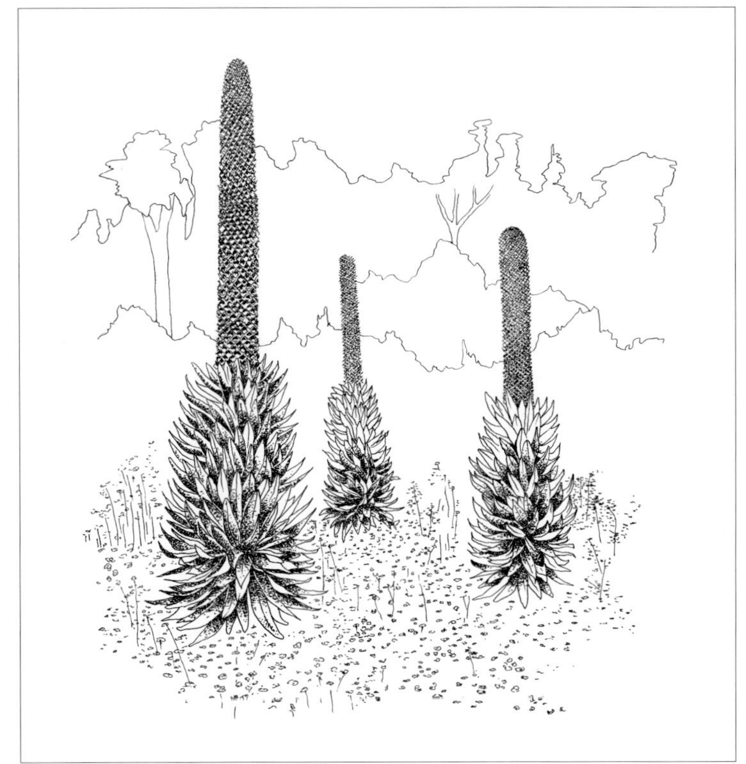

Lobelia gibberoa gradually give way to their kin *Lobelia lanuriensis*. Cabbage-like when immature, they turn into graceful mop-headed palms, before shooting their flowering spikes up to 8 metres towards the skies. *Rapanea rhododendroides* and *Hypericum*, or St John's Wort, appear among a greater variety of other plants on well-drained slopes. *Helichrysum guilelmii* are everlasting flowers, which grow in low shrubs. The loud cry of a Rwenzori Touraco may break the silence, but the spell of these enchanted forests is only reinforced when this large bird bursts in a flurry of brightly coloured green, blue and red feathers.

... AND BLACKISH BOGS

On level grounds, bogs form a serious obstacle for the trespasser. It takes a lot of skill to cross them without emerging all wet and muddy. The black peat absorbs the constant flow of precipitation and downtrickle from higher areas. The water is funnelled into underground rivulets, which surface from dark clefts, or gather in small ponds. These crystalline sources are eternally looking for a way out, downwards to the Nile. Sedges, mainly *Carex runsorroensis*, dominate the surface, interspersed with *Sphagnum* and other mosses. Over the years, the carex sedge builds up into a tough but flexible tussock. These formidable brush-headed stumps can become 1 metre high. The dullness of the carex boglands is broken by the most bizarre and emblematic plant of the Rwenzori: the *Lobelia bequaertii*. Purplish-green rosettes of immature plants sit together in small groups, while the flowering specimens stand tall as unworldly sentinels. Their phallic spikes can become 20 centimetres thick, and reach 3 metres high. The fast-growing, but ephemere columns have a repetitive pattern of sharply pointed bracts. Nature is outdoing the best of industrial design with this giant lobelia. No doubt the modernist photographer Karl Blossfeldt would have gone berserk with them. But whereas his photographs were strongly magnified to reveal the abstract beauty of plants, all you need here is the naked eye.

14

The face of the Afroalpine vegetation zone between 3,800 and 4,500 metres is greatly determined by giant groundsels, or *Senecio* trees. They have thick, leathery leaves, and a corky bark. Dead leaves stay attached to the stem, and form a dry, protective layer. Tree senecios may attain 7 to 8 metres in height, and form patches of fairly dense woodlands in well-watered or sheltered groves. On more open ground scattered specimens occur throughout the area. These individuals develop a much thicker coat of dried leaves. The bluish and elegant *Lobelia wollastonii* regularly intermingles with the senecios, appearing in small groups, or as stray loners. Of modest appearance, the *Alchemilla* scrub is another important member of the Afroalpine plant community. It occurs in various subspecies, and covers gentle slopes with a springy mat. Alchemilla is the principal food of the hyrax. This furry mammal is sometimes mistaken for a large guinea pig, but is actually closely related to the elephant! At night, they set off a series of shrill shrieks while feeding. The first time I unknowingly witnessed such a concert, I felt rather small lying in my tent near Skull Cave. Only in the morning my laughing porters enlightened me on the source of these ghostly cries in the darkness. Together with the red forest duiker, the hyrax constitutes the main menu of the leopard, who wanders up to 4,000 metres. Boglands, occupied by carex sedges, extend to this zone. But the most prolific vegetation of this altitudinal belt is formed by *Helichrysum*

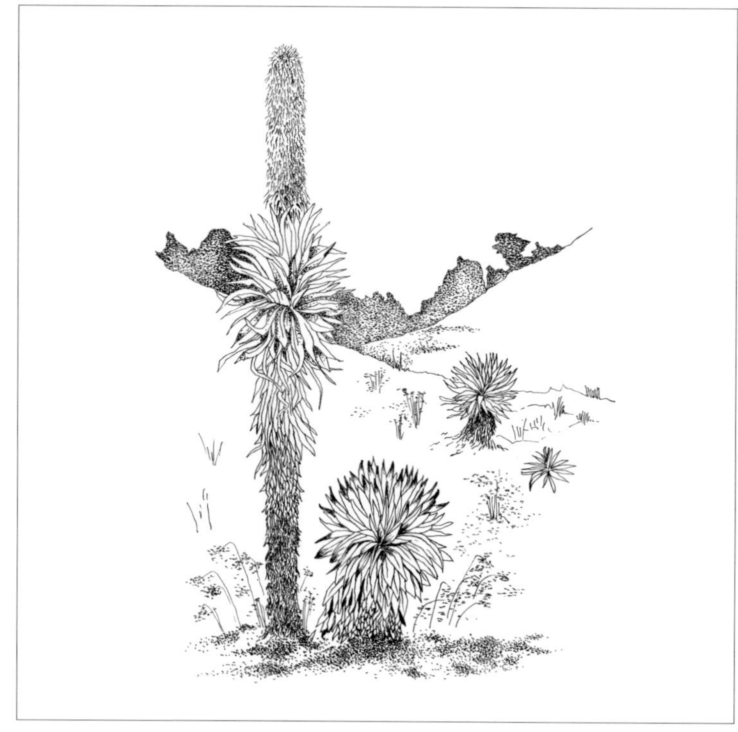

FIG. 6
Lobelia wollastonii

stuhlmanii. Its everlasting silvery white flowers open swiftly at every glance of the sun, closing again to protect the bud against colder conditions. At higher elevations it grows low and very open. But in lower parts, the helichrysum scrub becomes a dense thicket, reaching up to 2 metres high. Find me a shrubbery!

SUMMER EVERY DAY, WINTER EVERY NIGHT

All these wonderful vegetative life forms are the result of a fierce evolutional struggle to maintain themselves under particular and difficult conditions. The Afroalpine climate of the Rwenzori Mountains is determined by two geographical factors: they are close to the equator, and high above sea level. This has some important consequences.

As the altitude increases, temperatures drop. The air also grows thinner, provoking intense radiation, even on clouded days. During the day the incoming radiation of ultraviolet and infrared light is fierce, while at night the outward radiation under a clear sky has a considerable cooling effect. The equatorial location dictates marked diurnal variations in temperature, whereas the seasonal differences are less important. As the Swedish botanist Olov Hedberg puts it: "Summer every day, winter every night". Plants needed to adapt themselves in a specialised way to survive here.

PROFESSOR OLOV HEDBERG OF THE UNIVERSITY OF UPPSALA WAS A PIONEER IN THIS VIRGIN FIELD OF SCIENCE. OUR PRESENT KNOWL-EDGE OF THE AFROALPINE BIOSYSTEM OWES MUCH TO THE RESEARCH HE AND HIS WIFE INGA DID ON THE RWENZORI AND OTHER HIGH MOUNTAINS IN EASTERN AFRICA. HIS BREAKTHROUGH VIEWS WERE BASED ON THEIR SYSTEMATIC FIELDWORK IN THE LATE 1940S. *FEATURES OF AFROALPINE PLANT ECOLOGY* REMAINS A LANDMARK IN EQUATO-RIAL ALPINE ECOLOGICAL RESEARCH UP TILL TODAY, AND IS STILL AVAILABLE IN A FACSIMILE RE-EDITION OF 1995.

There is no water shortage in the Rwenzori. Yet several members of the Afroalpine family bear resemblance with species that normally thrive in desert climates. The reason lies in their similar water economy. Although abundantly present, water is not always readily available to the Afroalpine plants when they need it. The nightly frosts affect the sap transport in the plants, and the intake of water by its roots. As the day begins, the air temperature and radiation level rise rapidly, putting strenuous demands on the exposed parts of the plants. It is vital to meet the transpiration demands of the leaves, and maintain a proper water balance. To counter the effects of freezing, the Afroalpine plants have developed the insulation systems which give them such a striking appearance. As a rule, these adaptive trends become more prominent as the altitude increases.

The carex sedges and grasses insulate themselves and their underlying roots by forming dense tussocks. The energy these wads absorb during the day is released slowly at night. Cushion plants protect their stems in a similar way, while other species solve the problem of a frozen stem by not having one, their leaves forming a flat rosette lying directly on the ground.

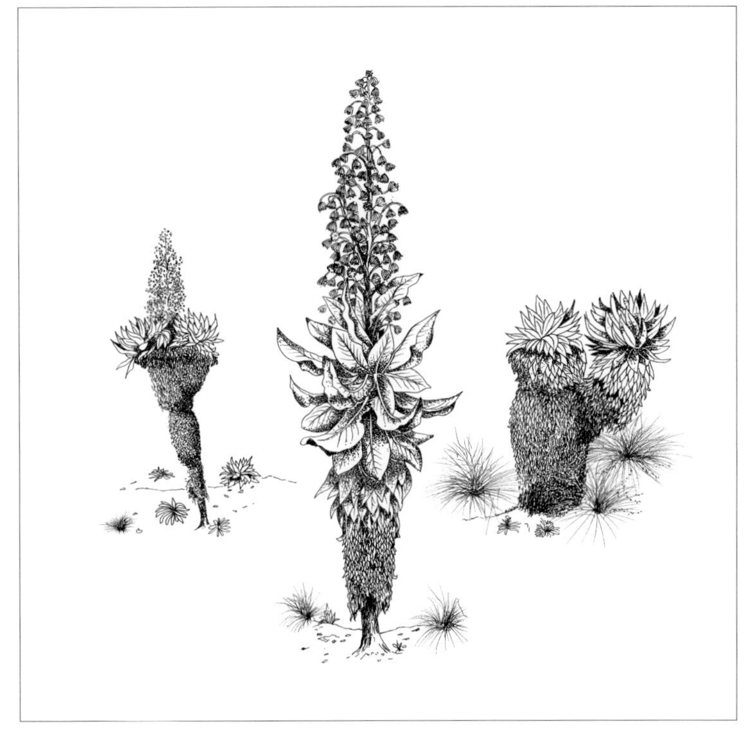

Scrubs like alchemilla and everlasting flowers are tackling the problem with their narrow and tough leaves. A silvery or hair-covered leaf provides more effective insulation, reducing overnight heat loss. By forming dense mats of shrub, they also temper nightly cooling in contrast to the unprotected bare soil surface.

While some plants seek refuge from the harsh conditions in miniaturism, others have taken to gigantism. Related species in temperate climates grow only a few centimetres high, but here the unlimited availability of water and sunlight have enabled the Afroalpine variants to reach huge proportions. This earned them the name "botanical big game", another famous quote by Olov Hedberg. Their sheer bulk offers a good degree of protection against the cold. The giant *Senecio adnivalis* starts as a cabbage-like rosette, which closes at night to protect the bud. The thick shiny leaves reflect a radiation overdose. Over the years the plant is gradually elevated by its slow-growing stem. Older leaves are replaced by new ones, but stay permanently attached to the plant. They form a

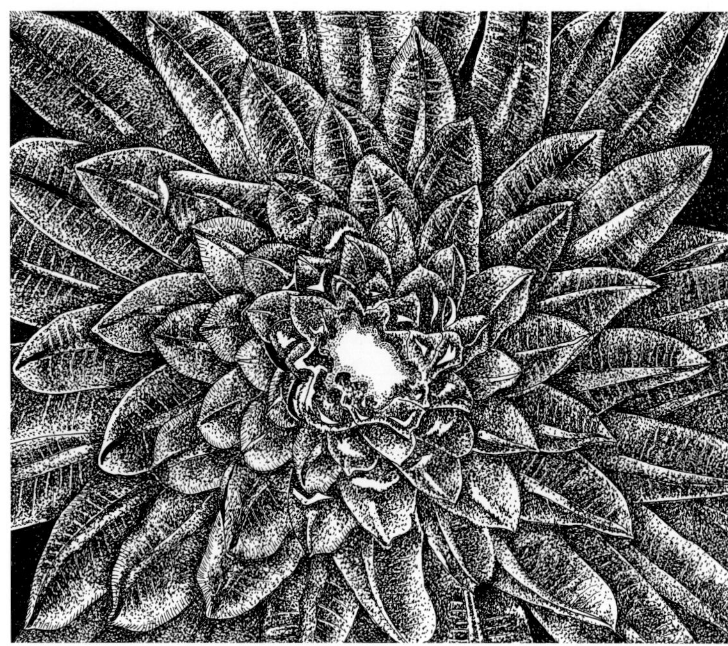

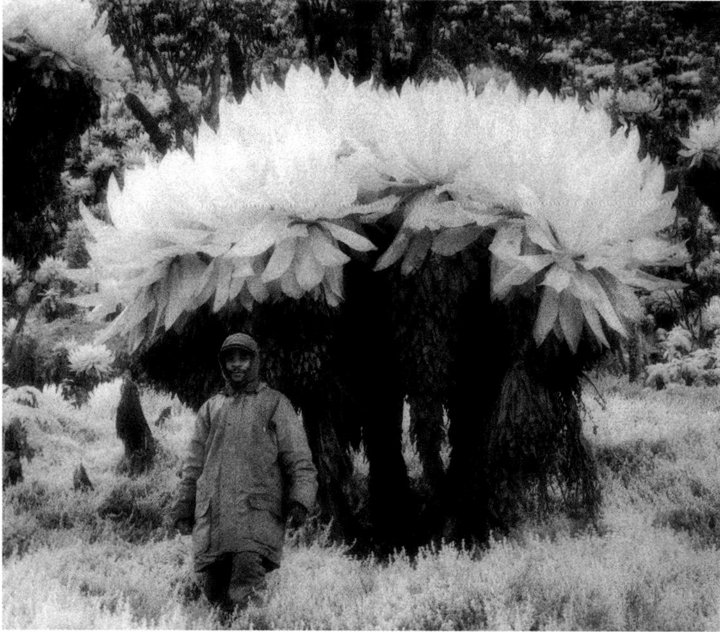

dry and shrivelled coat which effectively insulates the trunk. As the tree ages, this mantle is gradually replaced by a thick cork cortex. As a result, the water storage tissues inside do not get frozen. And when sun rises, the unfolding leaves can immediately draw all the sap they need. Senecio trees can become several hundreds of years old.

In a much similar way, the fast-growing giant lobelias are adept at coping with their environment. The leaf rosette of the *Lobelia bequaertii* closes tight at night to protect the growing bud. At dawn, it opens up swiftly to make the best of the day. The heart of the rosette acts as a small water reservoir. The surface of the fluid may be covered by a thin layer of ice in the morning, but the night is never long enough to freeze it completely. This is yet another device to prevent overnight damage to the underlying bud. The giant lobelias are monocarpic: for several years they gather energy reserves, till their time has come to flower and die. In a few months time, the *Lobelia bequaertii* shoots its formidable but feather-light column up towards the skies. Geometrically arranged bracts hide the hundreds of flowers from solar radiation, giving the stalk its amazing looks. The hollow

stem contains the sap reservoir which meets the plants demands at first light. The *Lobelia wollastonii* does it in a comparable way, but chooses to protect its flowering spike with a dense silvery hair cover. At lower altitudes the giant heathers and two other species of lobelias also grow spectacularly large. The *Lobelia gibberoa* and *lanuriensis* have elegant slim stems and a more open leaf rosette, less concerned as they are with insulation. Unhindered by a strenuous regime of nightly frosts, they seem indeed to take full advantage of the abundant ultraviolet light and rain.

A MOONLIGHT VISION

But this environment is much more than a botanist's playground. Only an insensitive man could ignore the enigmatic beauty of this primeval world. And yet there is still a lot to discover, not just by exploring remote and unvisited grounds, but also by trying new artistic paths. For there is a world of creative possibilities unseen by most visitors, because reality in itself is so overwhelming.
Yet this book is a documentary work. Although of a poetic nature, it reflects a vision on one of the few remaining areas on earth unspoiled

by human presence. It focuses on the mystical aura of Africa's Mountain s of the Moon in general, and of its Afroalpine vegetation in particular. I believe that herein lies the essence of this subject. Trying to visualise the spirit of this place is a way of exploring the boundaries of documentary photography.

For my flowers of the moon are no flowers in the true sense of the word. I wanted to photograph the afroalpine flora as a unique gift of nature, set against a monumental backdrop. Indeed the prehistoric landscapes of the Rwenzori are a formidable aula to encompass such an extravagant vegetation. Roughly, I photographed between 3,000 and 4,500 metres in altitude. By having the spectator lose all sense of proportion and making abstraction of colour, I hope to show these plants as biological sculptures. Sometimes this way of representation was reinforced by the pedestal of mosses on which some particularly enchanting specimens were growing. As if some higher power was indeed proudly exhibiting its finest creations, reflecting an otherworldly image of Africa.

The choice of infrared black-and-white photography causes a weird moonlight vision, which enhances the pristine beauty of these landscapes. Often discarded by "serious" photographers as a hat-trick from art-school students and amateur photographers, I found it to be the right way to express my view. The use of this film has some particular consequences. Blue skies are rendered into a dramatic black, while the texture of clouds and mists is accentuated. Water, absorbing the infrared radiation, is also hurled into darkness. But most striking is the effect on the vegetation. As the chlorophyll of a leaf tends to reflect most of the infrared radiation, it is registered in light tones. Considering the quantity of infrared radiation in the Afroalpine realm, this outcome plays a prominent role in this work. The black-and-white prints radiate the light captured by the extraordinary flora of these legendary Mountains of the Moon. However estranging an effect this may have, this is not an imaginary world. That is remarkable in times where the real natural environment is progressively being destroyed, and where virtual reality takes over.

ECOLOGICAL PRESERVATION

In the 1930s the Congolese slopes of the Rwenzori became a national park, and the Belgians started to construct an excellent chain of mountain huts on that side. A similar hut system was erected on the Ugandan territory after World War II. Only in 1991 did this part also become a national park. Over the years, the trickle of visitors has increased, sometimes interrupted by guerrilla warfare and rebel intrusions. Nowadays several hundreds of tourists and climbers visit the range every year, accompanied by a tenfold of Konzo guides and porters. High entrance fees and the physical demands of trekking in the Rwenzori restrict the development of mass tourism. Yet the present eco-tourism has a considerable impact on the fragile environment. The vegetation in the bogs gets

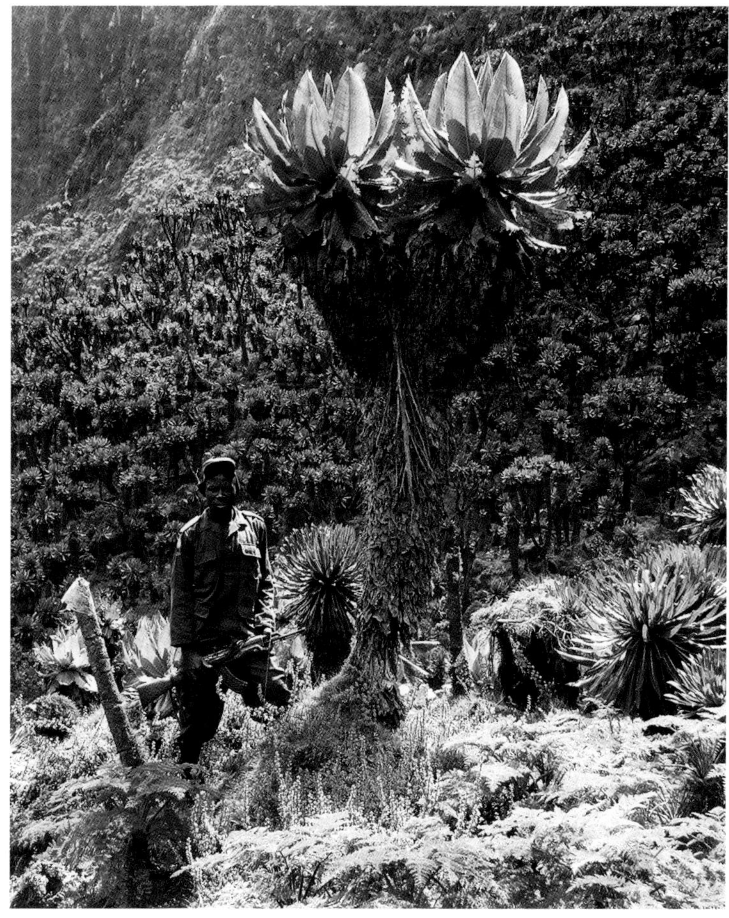

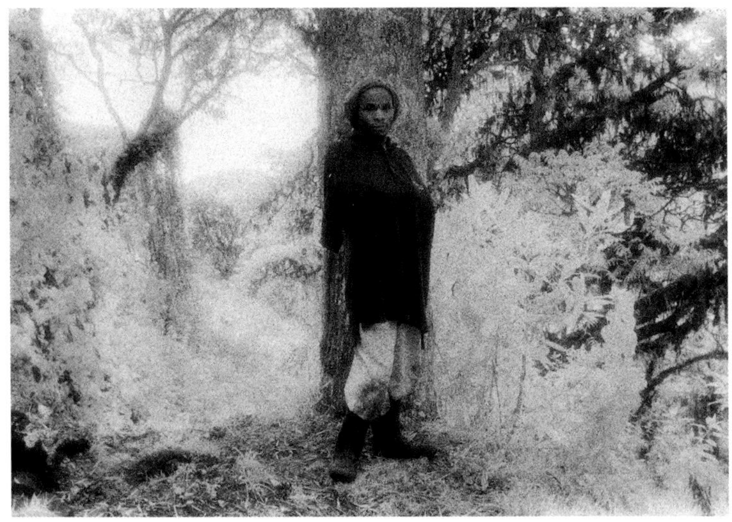

GUY YEOMAN IS THE AUTHOR OF *AFRICA'S MOUNTAINS OF THE MOON*, A SUPERB ACCOUNT OF HIS EXTENSIVE TRAVELS IN THE RWENZORI AND ADJACENT REGIONS. IT EVOKES THIS MENACED UNIVERSE IN A COMPELLING WAY AND PLACES IT IN THE WIDER CONTEXT OF ECOLOGICAL PRESERVATION IN AFRICA. YEOMAN FIRST VISITED THE REGION IN WORLD WAR II AS A BRITISH OFFICER, AND AFTERWARDS WORKED FOR TWELVE YEARS AS A VETERINARIAN IN PRESENT TANZANIA. HIS OWN FIELD EXPERIENCE LED HIM TO BELIEVE THAT MOST OF THE WELL-INTENDED WESTERN AID HAS DONE MORE HARM THAN GOOD TO THE CONTINENT AND ITS INHABITANTS. A MOUNTAIN CABIN IN THE RWENZORI HAS BEEN NAMED AFTER HIM.

trampled, and not surprisingly porters cut firewood against regulations. I would do the same to warm myself in a rock-shelter, poorly dressed and tired after a day of hauling equipment for Gore-tex-clad clients. The dilemma is that the tourist incomes are much needed to preserve the park and sustain local populations, while their passage stresses the ecosystem by damaging it.

In 1994 the Rwenzori National Park was inscribed on the UNESCO World Heritage list. This declaration offers a certain degree of protection against the advancing deforestation. But in the long run, overpopulation will guarantee the total denudation of forest up to the highest level at which food can be grown or firewood extracted. According to Guy Yeoman the problems facing the Rwenzori call for a much wider approach. They cannot be solved without addressing the basic problems of Africa as a whole. The conservation of the Rwenzori from further encroachment, and future protection of the whole range will depend on the people themselves and not on Western ideas and donor funding. Only a sustainable and organic balance between the interests of local population and the preservation of the ecosystem will offer a long-term perspective.

Another major threat to this unique environment is also caused by humans, but comes from above. Global warming and greenhouse effect are rapidly melting away the glaciers, which are a keystone to the existence of this ecosystem. The Rwenzori glaciers were first surveyed a century ago by the Duke of the Abruzzi expedition. The total glaciated surface was estimated to be around seven square kilometres. With less than one square kilometre of glacier ice remaining, extrapolation of this trend leads us to expect the icecaps of the Rwenzori will disappear within the next two decades. According to scientist Richard Taylor, tropical glaciers are very sensitive indicators of climate change.

HYDROLOGIST RICHARD TAYLOR OF THE UNIVERSITY COLLEGE OF LONDON AND HIS BRITISH-UGANDAN EXPEDITION TEAM HAVE BEEN RESEARCHING GLACIAL RETREAT ON THE RWENZORI. HIS CONCLUSIONS CONFIRM THE IRONY THAT AFRICA WILL PROBABLY SUFFER MOST OF THE CONSEQUENCES OF CLIMATE CHANGE, WHILE THE CONTINENT'S SHARE IN GLOBAL GREENHOUSE GAS EMISSION IS NEGLIGIBLE.

If a quick halt to this process can effectively be brought about, we should not ignore this kind of warning to the danger that looms over planet earth, our only home. The question is: will it survive the rising tide of mankind?

BIBLIOGRAPHY

Applied Infrared Photography, Eastman Kodak Co., 1977.

ADAM, Hans-Christian, *Karl Blossfeldt*. Cologne: Taschen, 1999.

DE FILIPPI, Filippo, *Il Ruwenzori*. Milan: Hoepli, 1908.

ELSE, David, *Trekking in East Africa*. Lonely Planet, 2003.

HEDBERG, Olov, *Afroalpine Vascular Plants – A Taxonomic Revision*. Uppsala: Almqvist & Wiksells Boktryckeri, 1957.

HEDBERG, Olov, *Features of Afroalpine Plant Ecology*. facsimile edition, Uppsala: Uppsala University, 1995.

LINDER, Peter and GEHRKE, Berit, *Common plants of the Rwenzori, particularly the upper zones*, 2006 (www.systbot.unizh.ch).

MANTOVANI, Roberto, *The Ruwenzori discovery: Luigi Amedeo di Savoia duca degli Abruzzi*. Turin: Museo Nazionale della Montagna, 1996.

PLUTH, David, *Uganda Rwenzori, a Range of Images*, Little Wolf Press, 1996.

OSMASTON, Henry, *Guide to the Rwenzori*. The Rwenzori Trust, 2006.

STANLEY, Henry Morton *Through the Dark Continent*. London: Sampson Low, Marston & Company, 1878.

STANLEY, Henry Morton, *In darkest Africa*. New York: Charles Scriber's Sons, 1890.

TAYLOR, Richard, *The son of the snow is angry - loss of glaciers threatens indigenous culture* (in: *The New Internationalist*, vol. 378, p. 6), 2005.

TAYLOR, Richard, MILEHAM, Lucinda, TINDIMUGAYA, Callist, MAJUGU, Andrea, NAKILEZA, Bob,

MUWANGA, Abushan, *Recent glacial recession in the Rwenzori Mountains of East Africa due to rising air temperature* (in: *Geophysical Research Letters*, vol. 33), 2006.

WIELOCHOWSKI, Andrew, *Map and Guide to the Rwenzori*, Llandovery: EWP, Haul Fryn, Cyclycwm, 1989.

YEOMAN, Guy, *Africa's Mountains of the Moon*. London: Elm Tree Books, 1989.

BIOGRAPHY

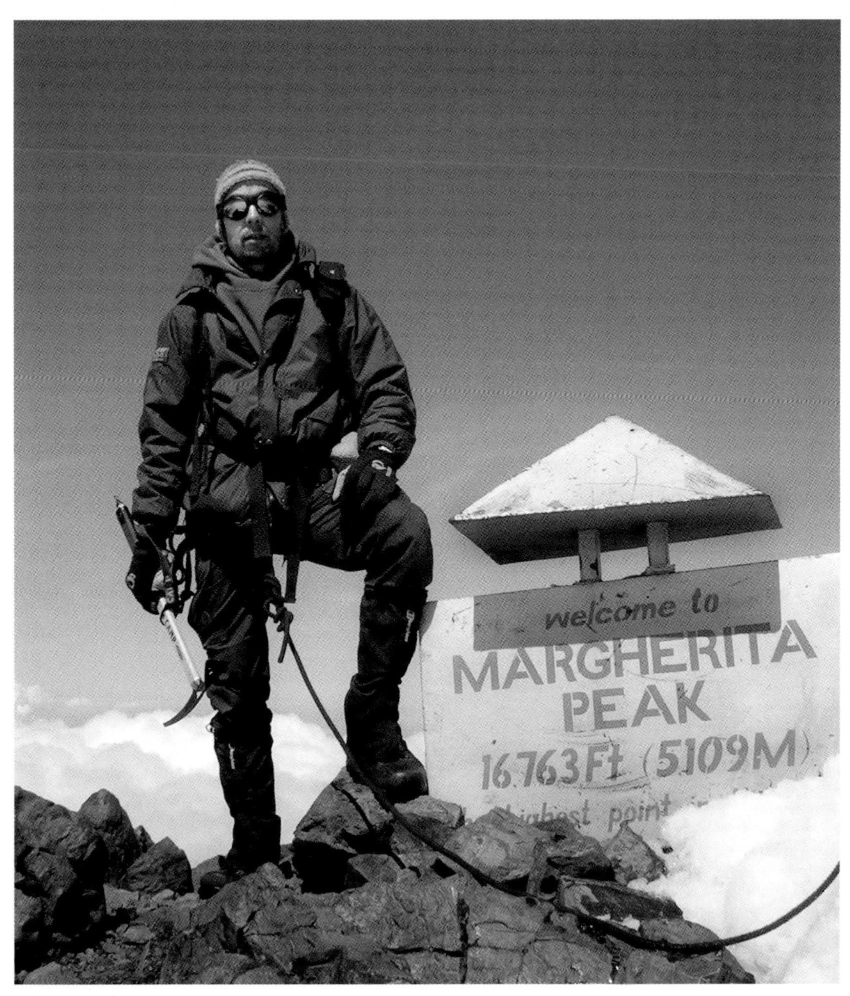

Sebastian Schutyser was born in Bruges in 1968. He spent his childhood in Zaïre (present-day Congo). After taking a degree in political science at the University of Ghent, he decided to study photography at the Royal Academy of Fine Arts in the same town. In 1996–97 he cycled across Mali and realised a series of portraits. This work earned him a grant from the Belgian Vocation Foundation. Since 1998, Schutyser has dedicated himself to doing a photographic survey of the adobe mosques of the Inner Niger Delta in Mali. After receiving a prize from the Friends of UNESCO (at the 13th national open photographic award), the Aga Khan Trust for Culture sponsored the completion of this work. It was subsequently published by 5 Continents Editions in 2003. His photographs were exhibited in Brussels at the Royal Africa Museum (2000); in the Netherlands at the Noorderlicht Photography Festival (2000); in Paris at the Maison Européenne de la Photographie (2002); in Frankfurt at the Deutsches Architekturmuseum (2003); in Mali at the Rencontres de la Photographie Africaine de Bamako, and at the Great Mosque of Djenné (2003); again in Brussels at BOZAR (2005); and recently in Korea at the Clayarch Gimhae Museum (2007). In 2004 he was awarded the € 25.000 Golden Clover grant from the Belgian Vocation Foundation for his work in Africa. Since his photographic expeditions to the Rwenzori Mountains in 2004 and 2005, he has been working on new projects in Africa, Europe and central Asia.

1. Portal Peaks
2. Rock formation near Bujongolo
3. Lake Bujuku
4. Mount Baker
5. Mubuku River
6. Giant heather (*Erica*) draped with Old Man's Beard (*Usnea*)
7. *Erica* forest
8. Dense vegetation near Bigo Bog
9. *Senecio adnivalis* on a carpet of *Alchemilla*
10. Flowering *Lobelia bequaertii*
11. *Senecio* forest
12. Bujuku River # 1
13. Giant groundsel in heather forest
14. *Helichrysum stuhlmannii* # 1
15. *Carex runssoroensis* grass tussock
16. *Senecio erici-rosenii* framing Mount Emin
17. *Senecio adnivalis* # 1
18. *Alchemilla* and *Helichrysum* scrub, *Senecio* woodland
19. Old Man's Beard hanging from heather trees
20. Mugusu valley
21. Upper Kitandara Lake
22. *Senecio adnivalis* on a pedestal of mosses (*Sphagnum*)
23. *Lobelia wollastonii* and *Senecio adnivalis*
24. *Lobelia lanuriensis*
25. Flowering *Lobelia wollastonii*
26. Mount Speke
27. Fallen groundsel tree and frozen pond at Irene Lakes
28. Giant groundsels and ferns # 1

29. Giant groundsels and ferns # 2
30. Riverine vegetation
31. *Senecio erici-rosenii*
32. Mosses and dripping water # 1
33. Mosses and dripping water # 2
34. Flowering *Lobelia bequaertii*, *Alchemilla* scrub (foreground), and *Erica* forest (background)
35. *Lobelia bequaertii*, before and after flowering
36. Lac du Speke (Speke Lake)
37. *Lobelia bequaertii*
38. *Helichrysum stuhlmannii* # 2
39. *Lobelia wollastonii*
40. *Senecio adnivalis* # 2
41. Lac de la Lune (Moon Lake) # 1
42. Kabamba Falls
43. Moss-heather forest
44. Dense vegetation on Bujuku River
45. *Senecio adnivalis* and *Lobelia wollastonii* near Leopard's Liar
46. Bujuku River # 2
47. Everlasting flowers *Helichrysum guilelmii*
48. *Senecio* tree overgrown with mosses
49. Rock in Lake Bujuku
50. Akendahi
51. Butawu Valley
52. Mount Stanley
53. Lac de la Lune (Moon Lake) # 2
54. Stuhlman Pass
55. *Senecio adnivalis* # 3

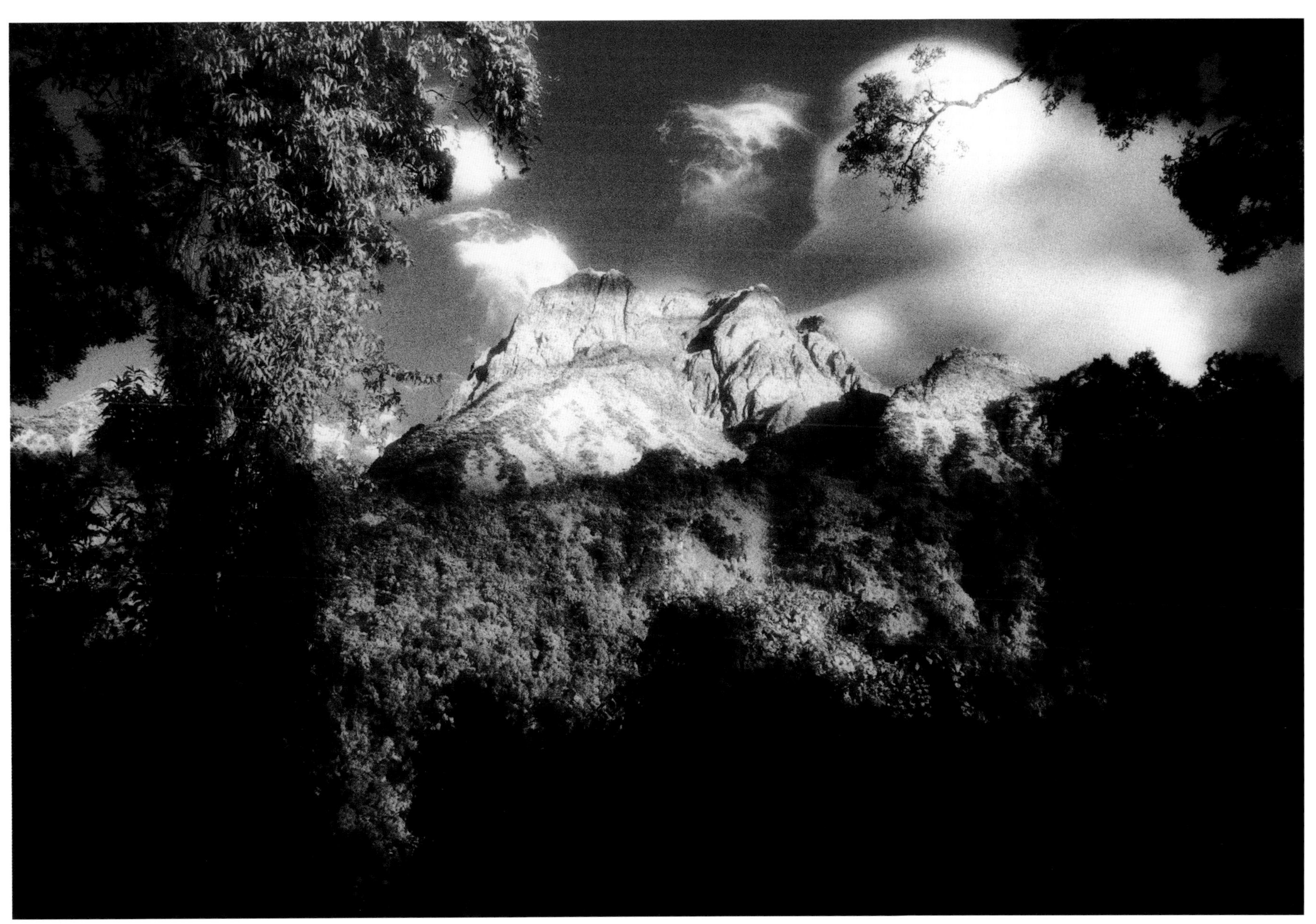

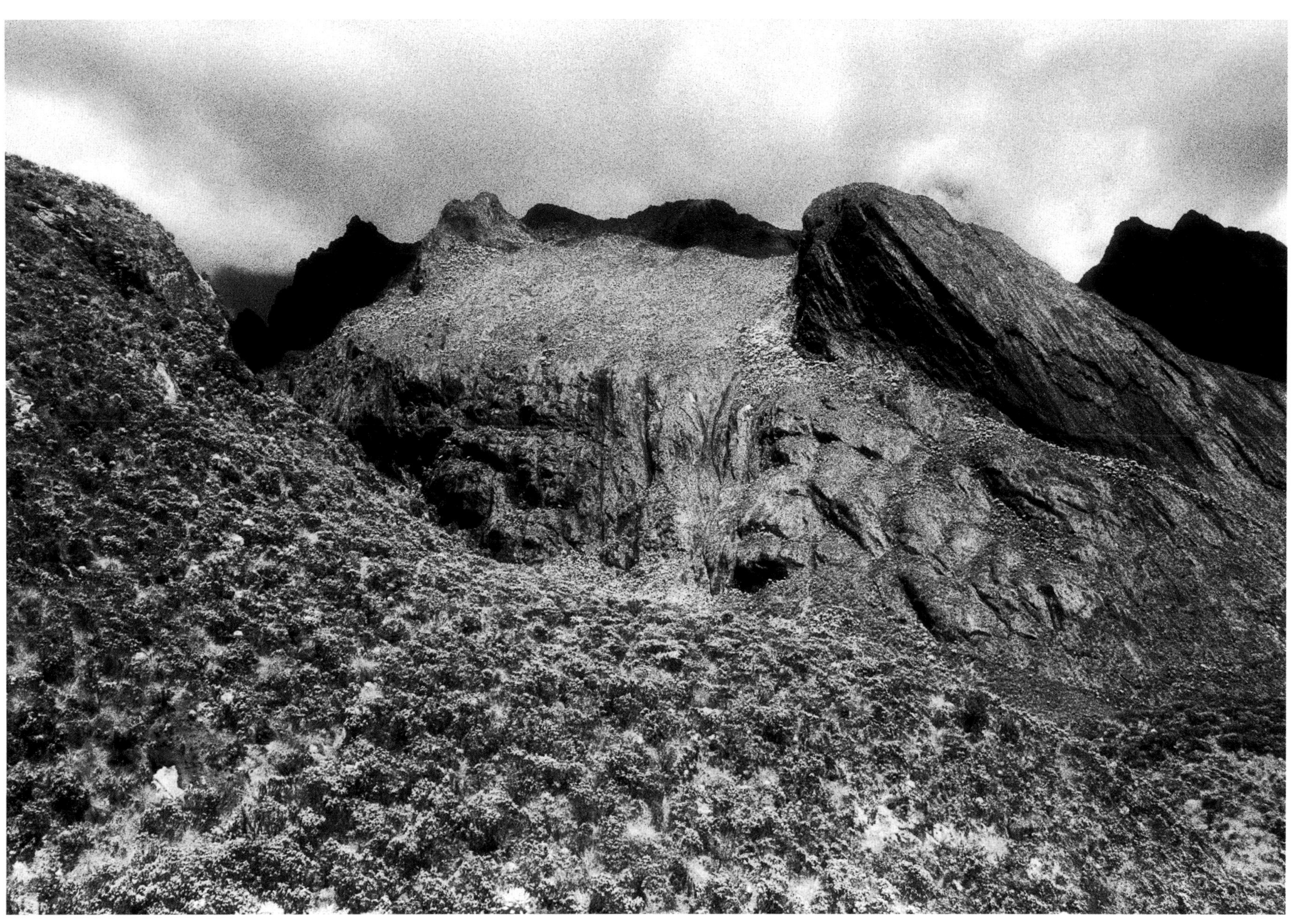

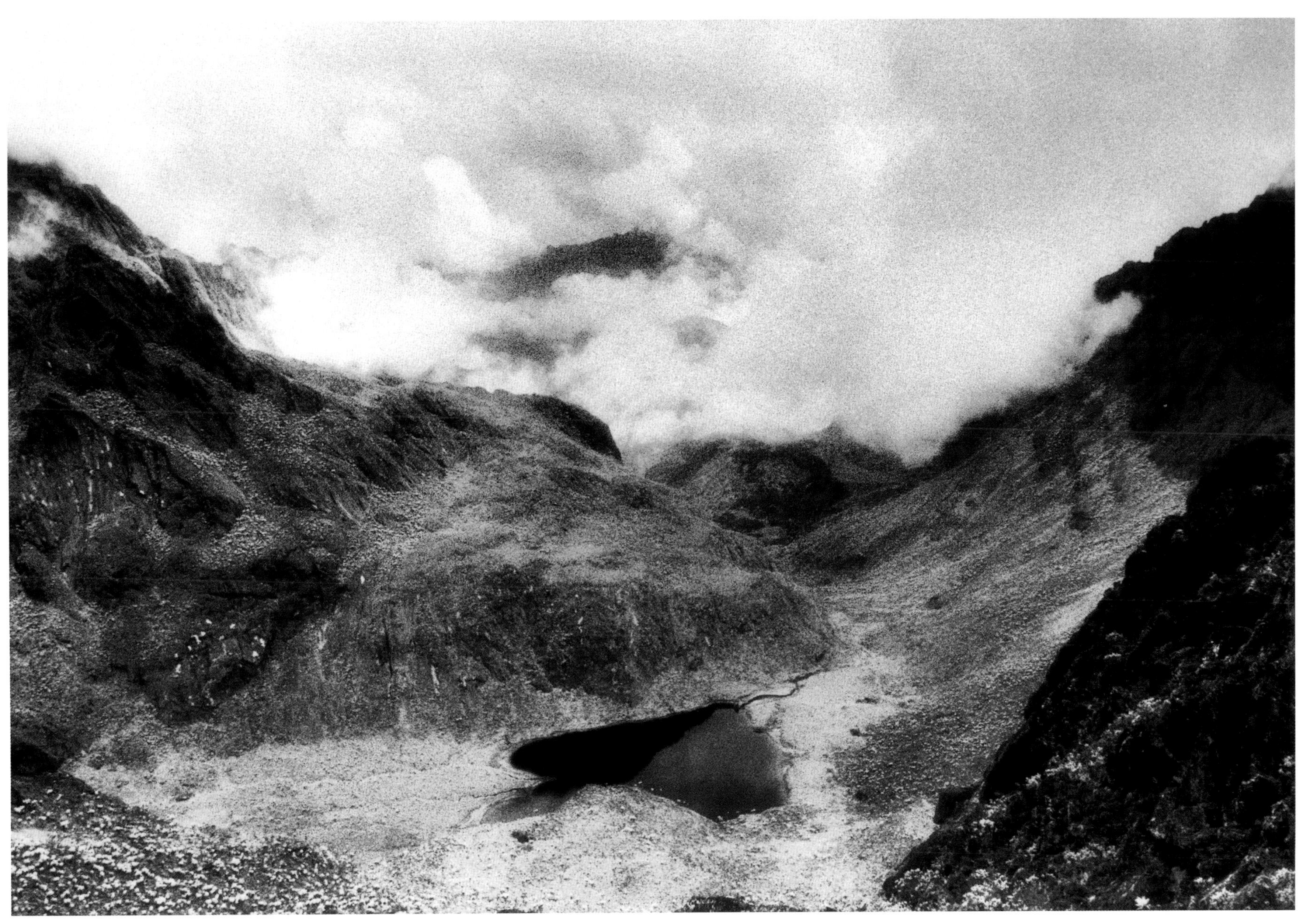

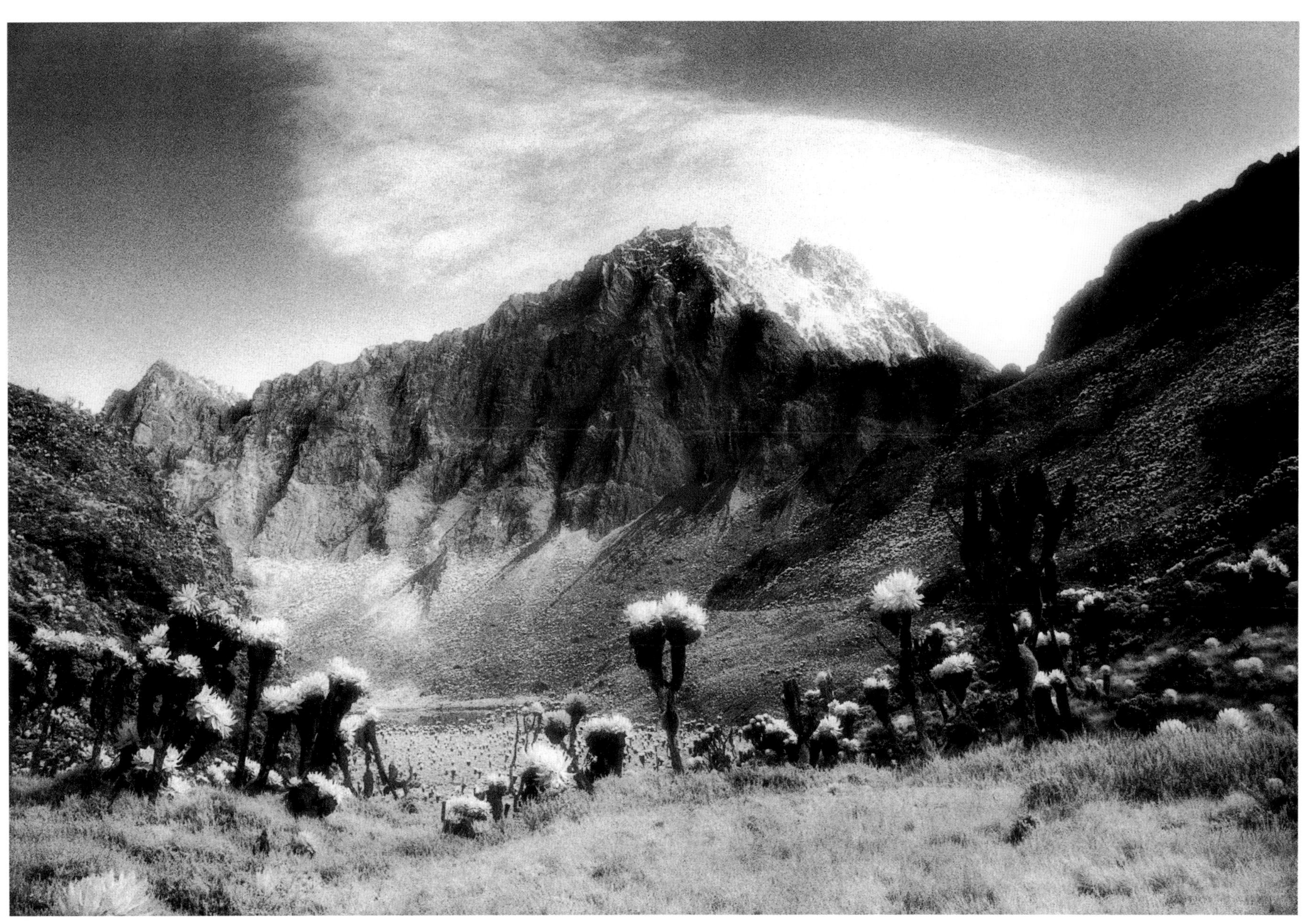

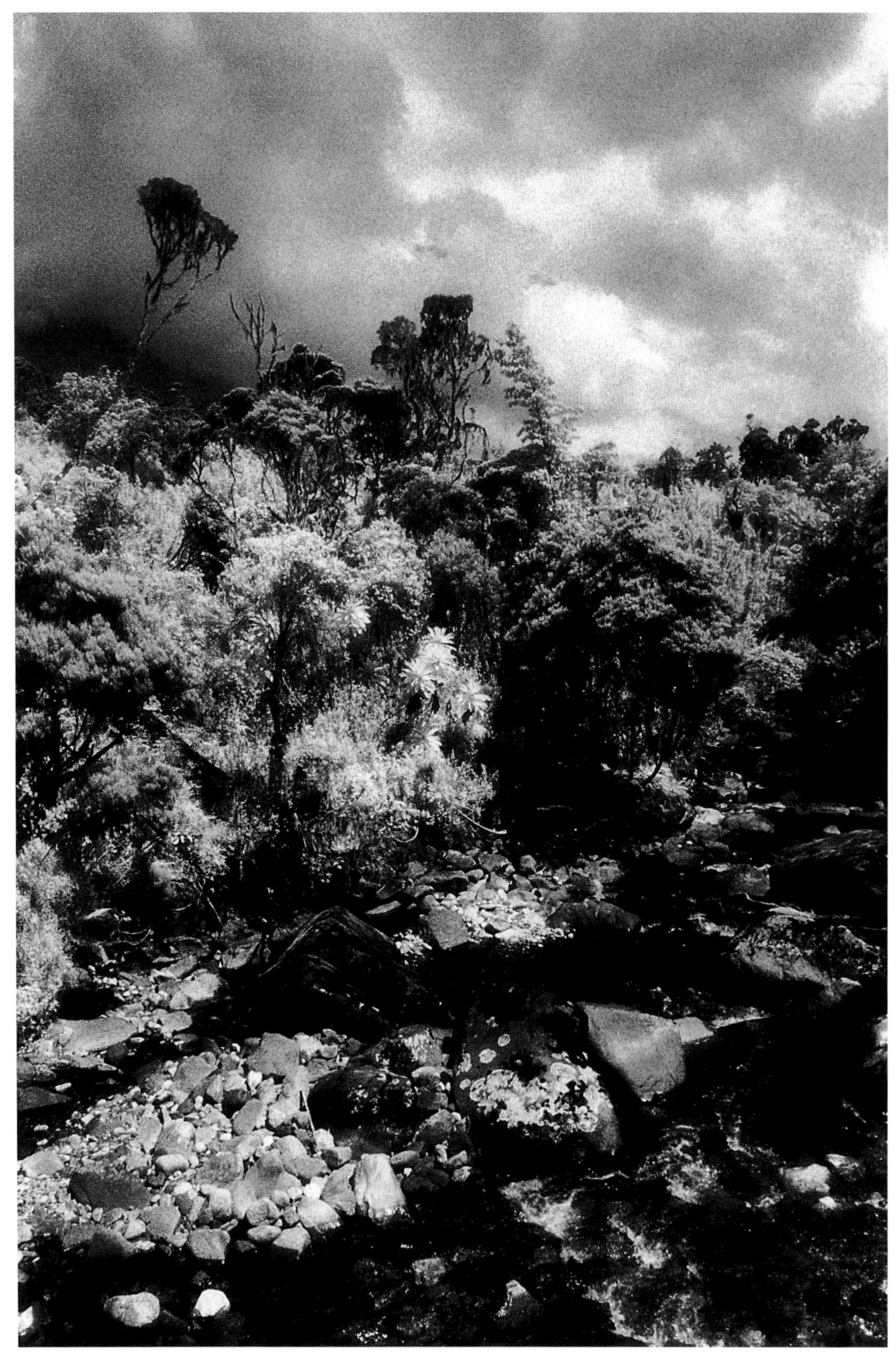

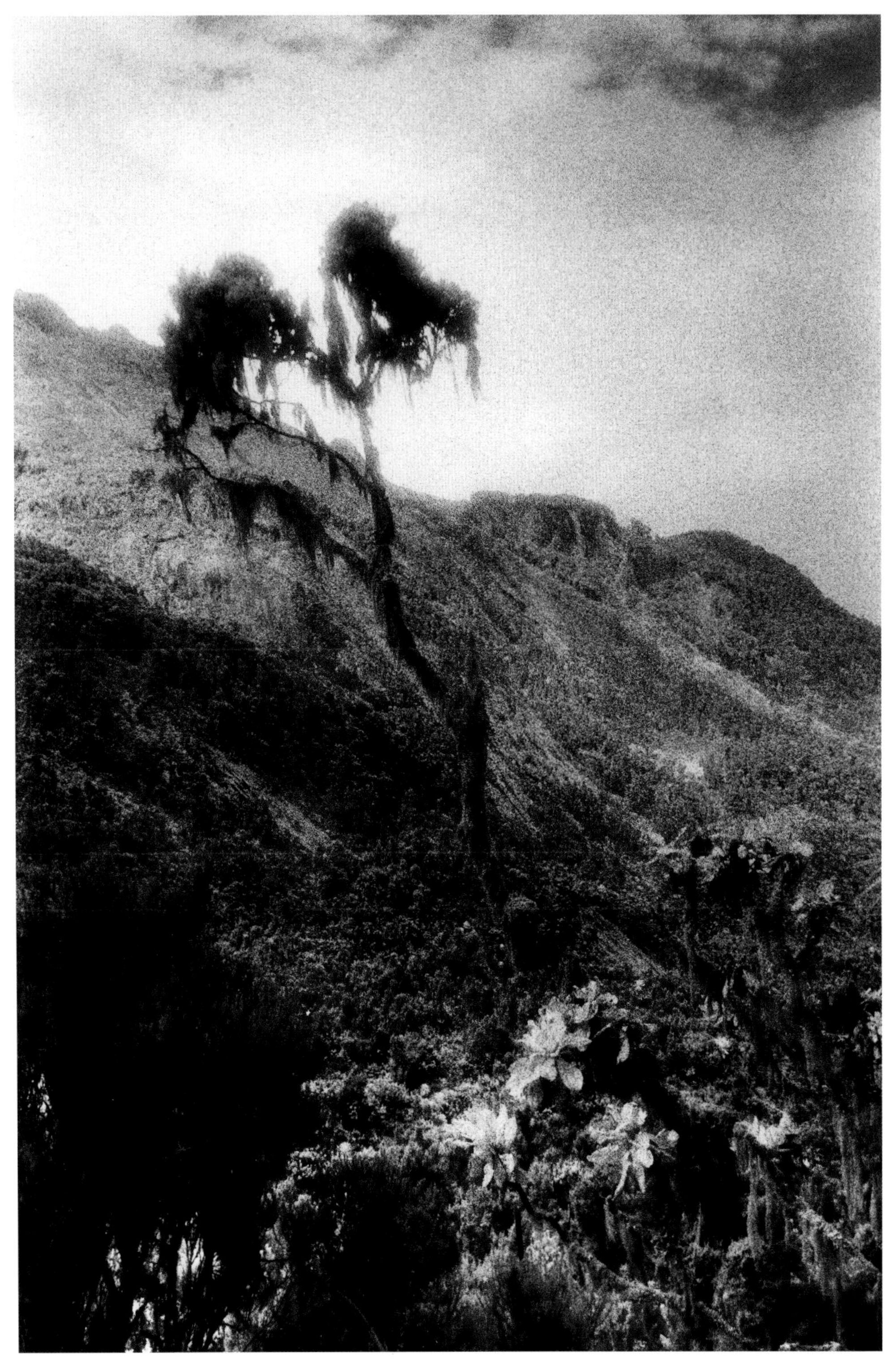

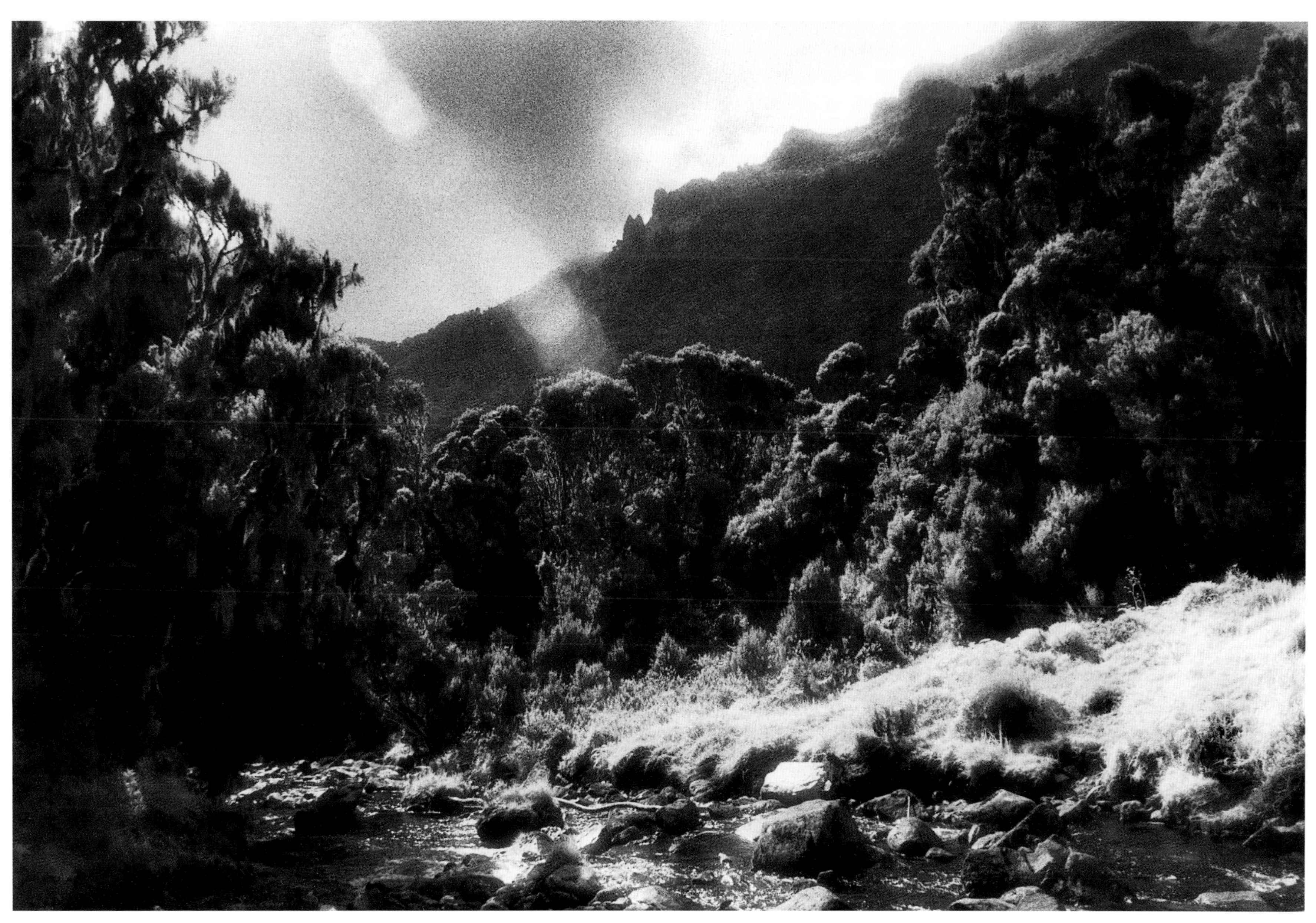

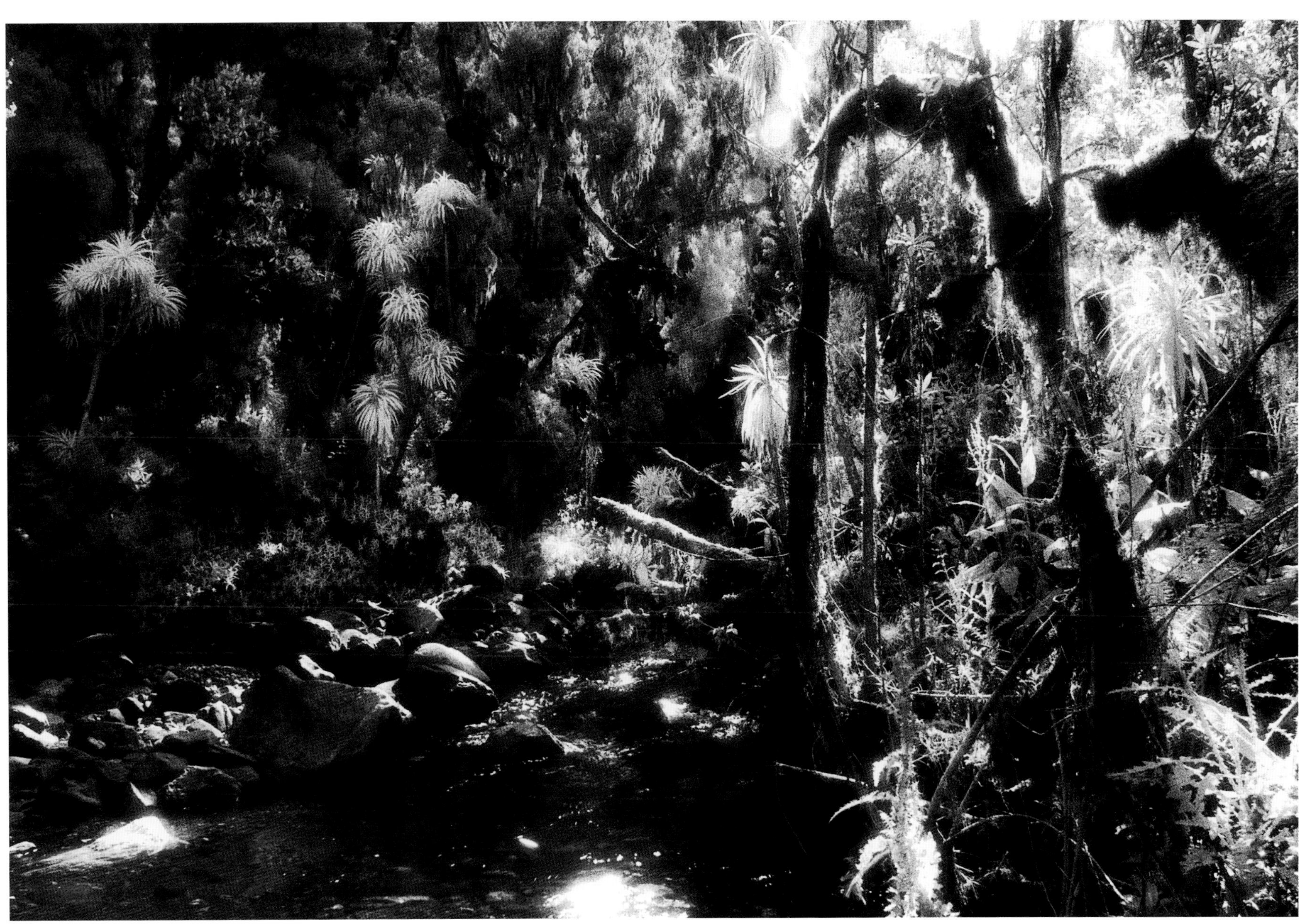

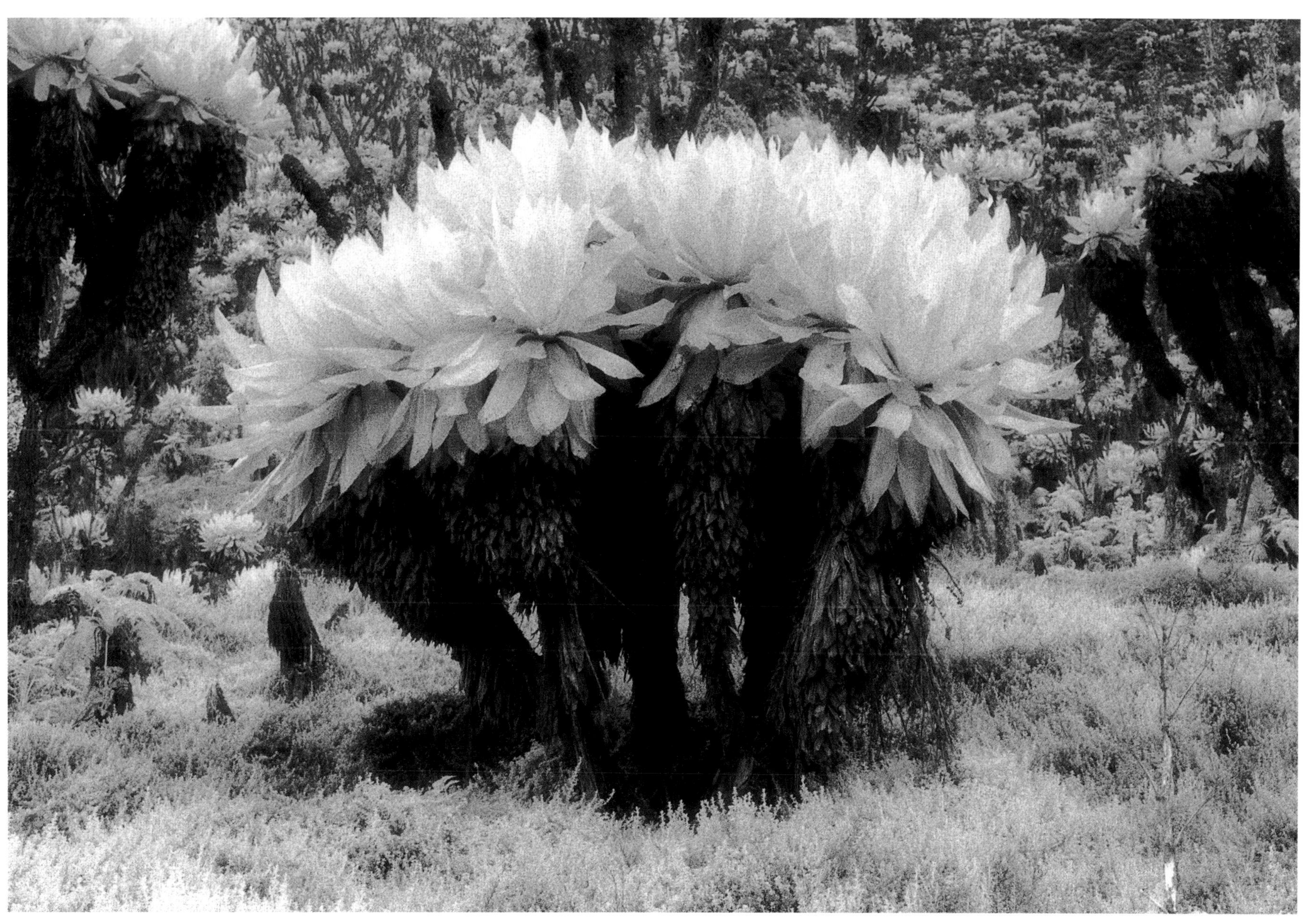

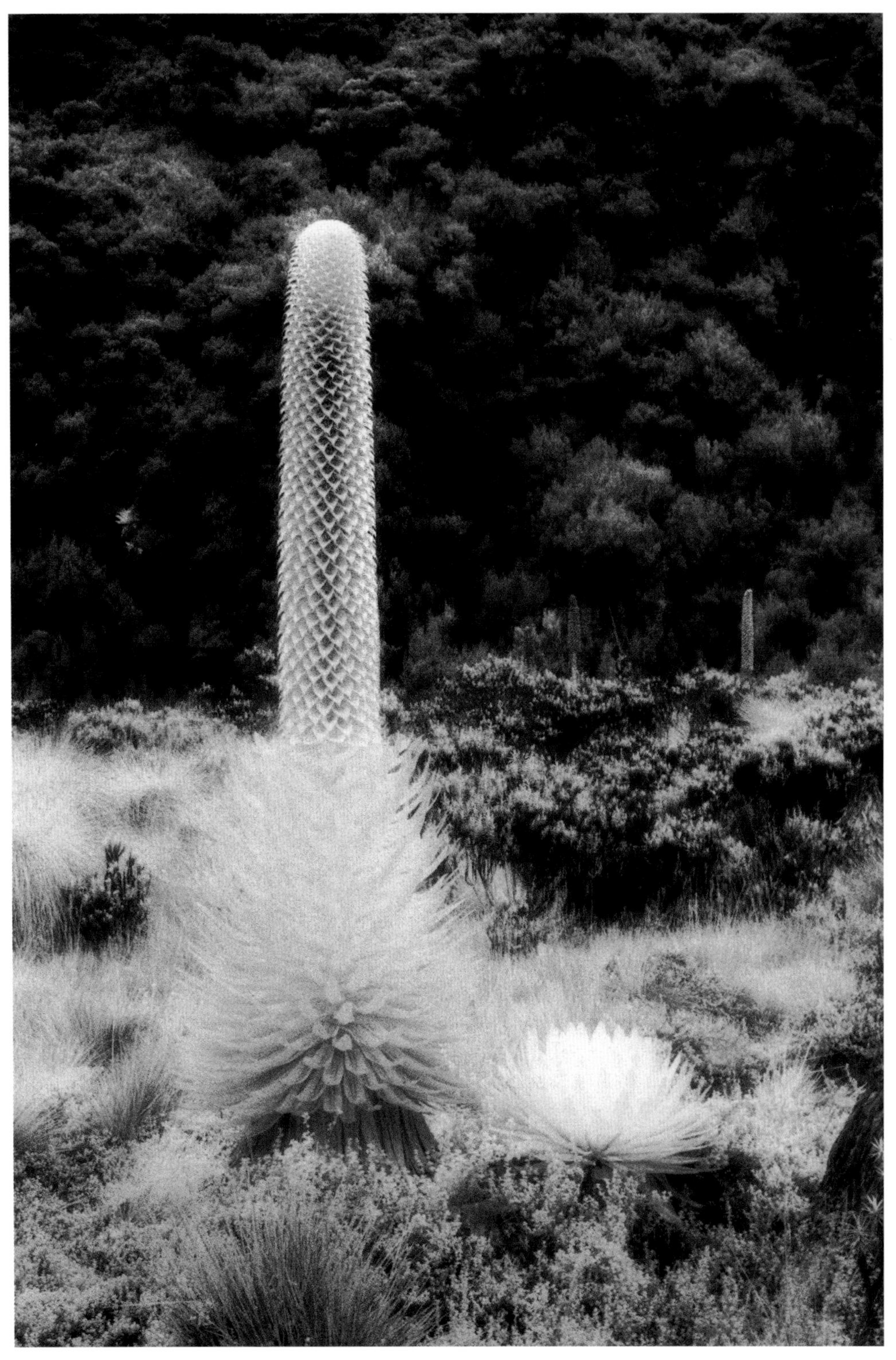

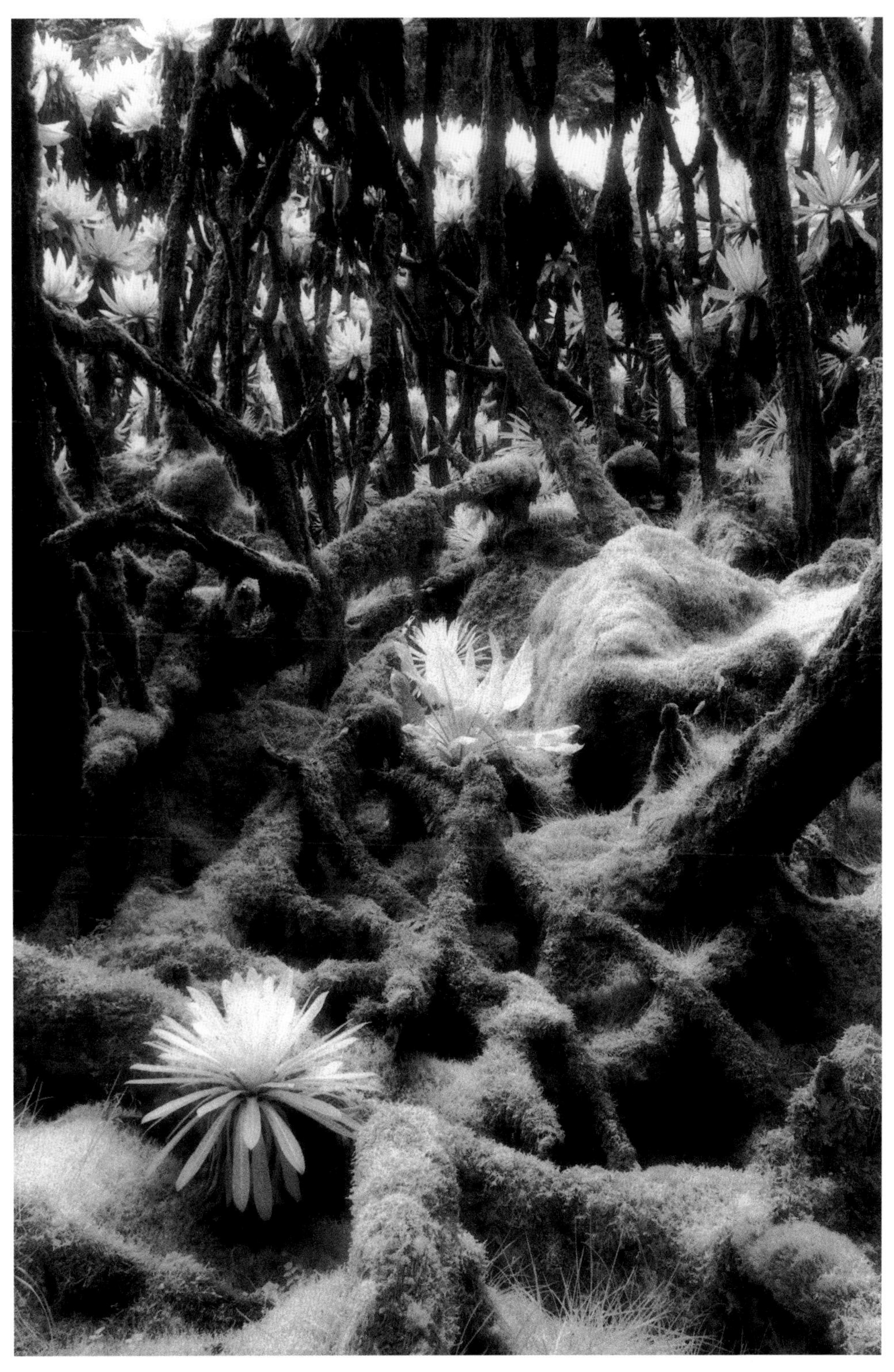

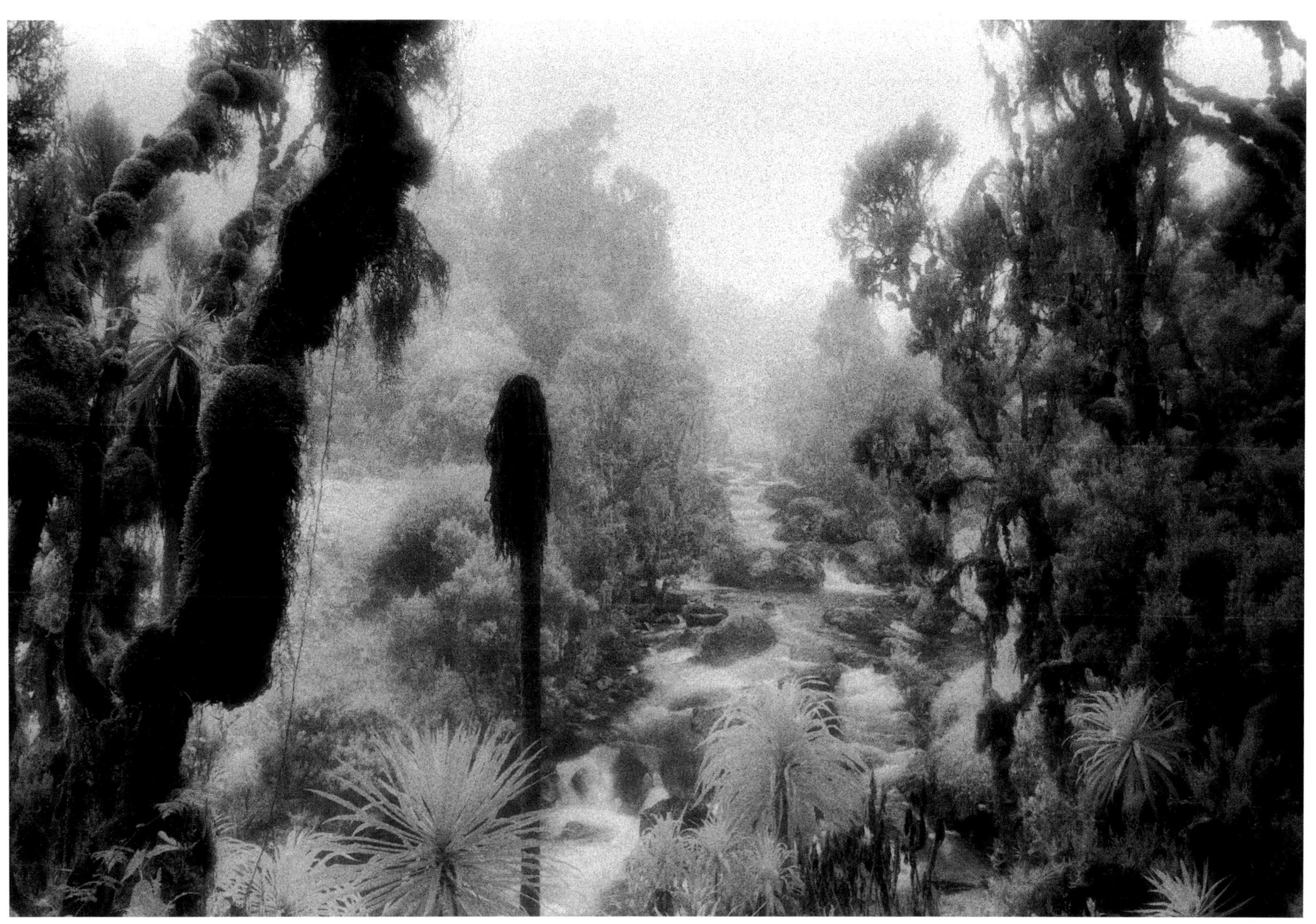

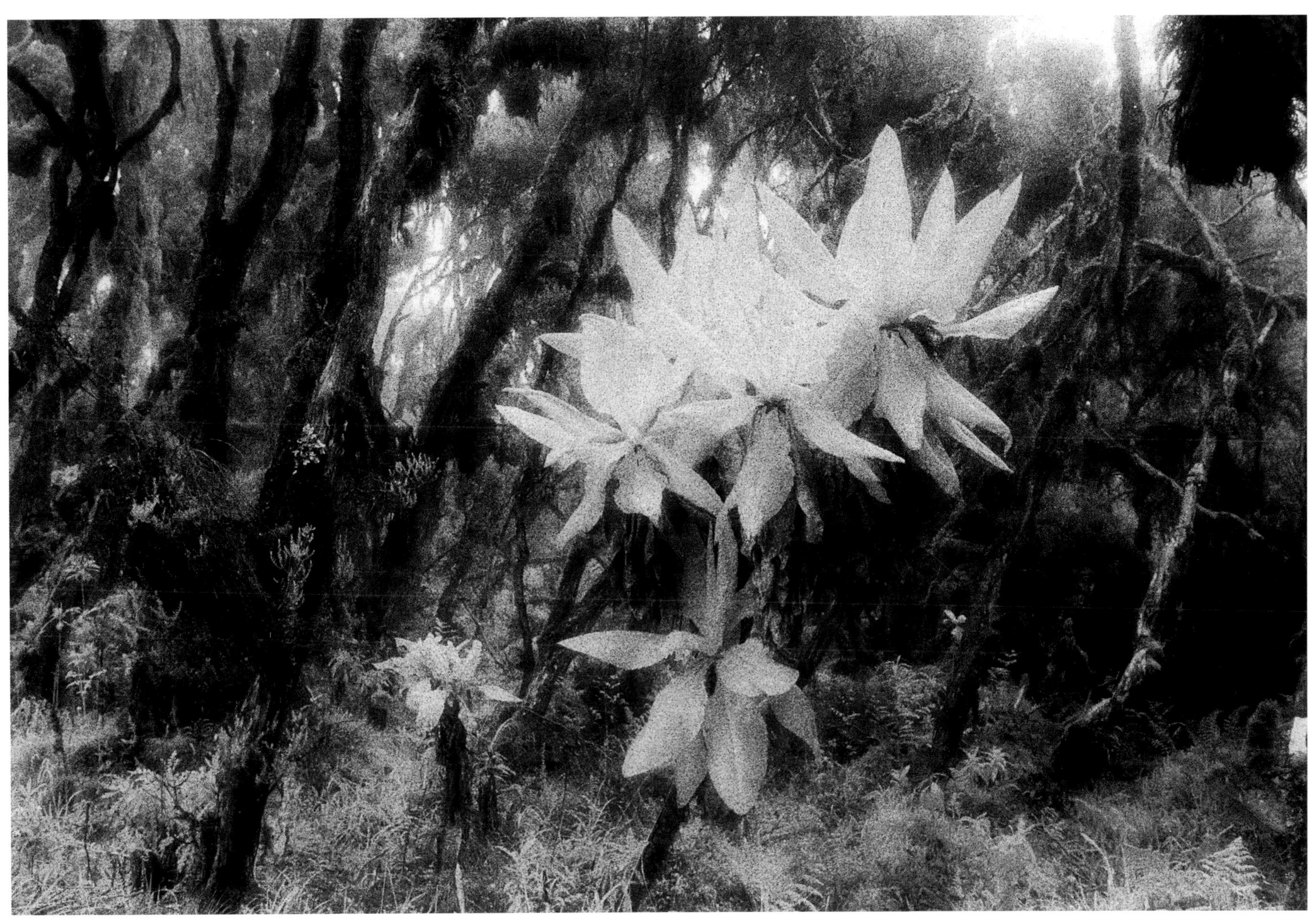

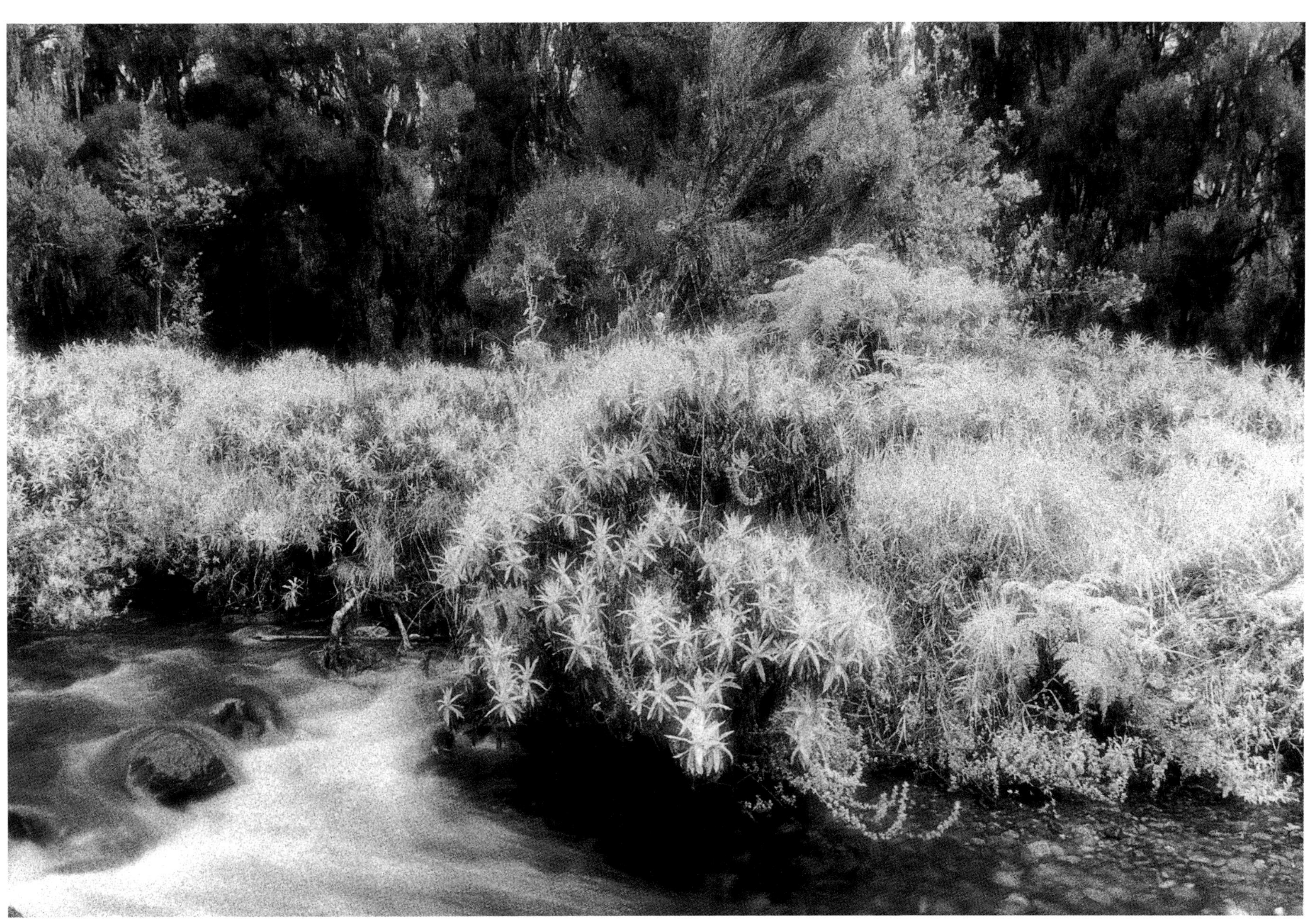

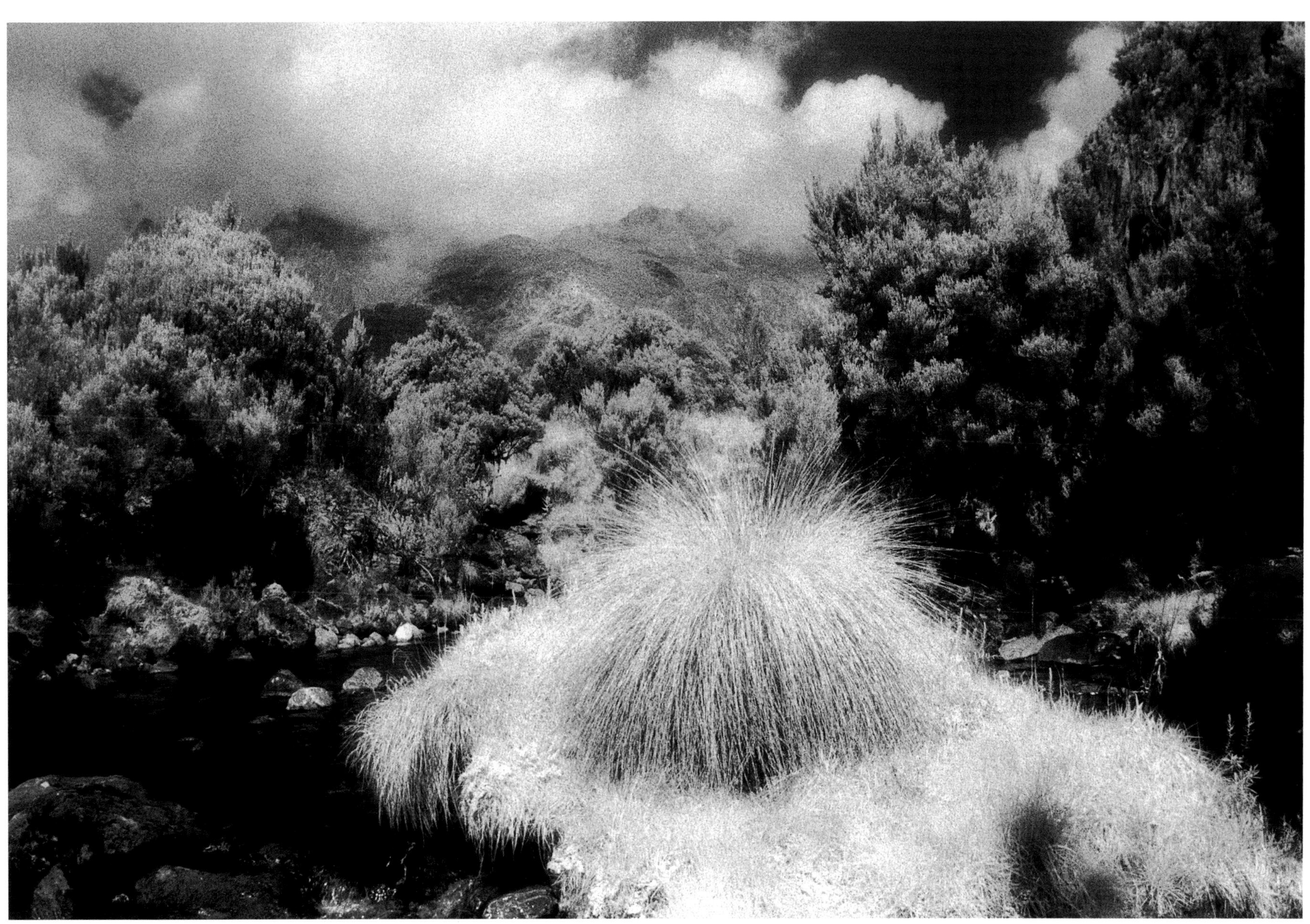

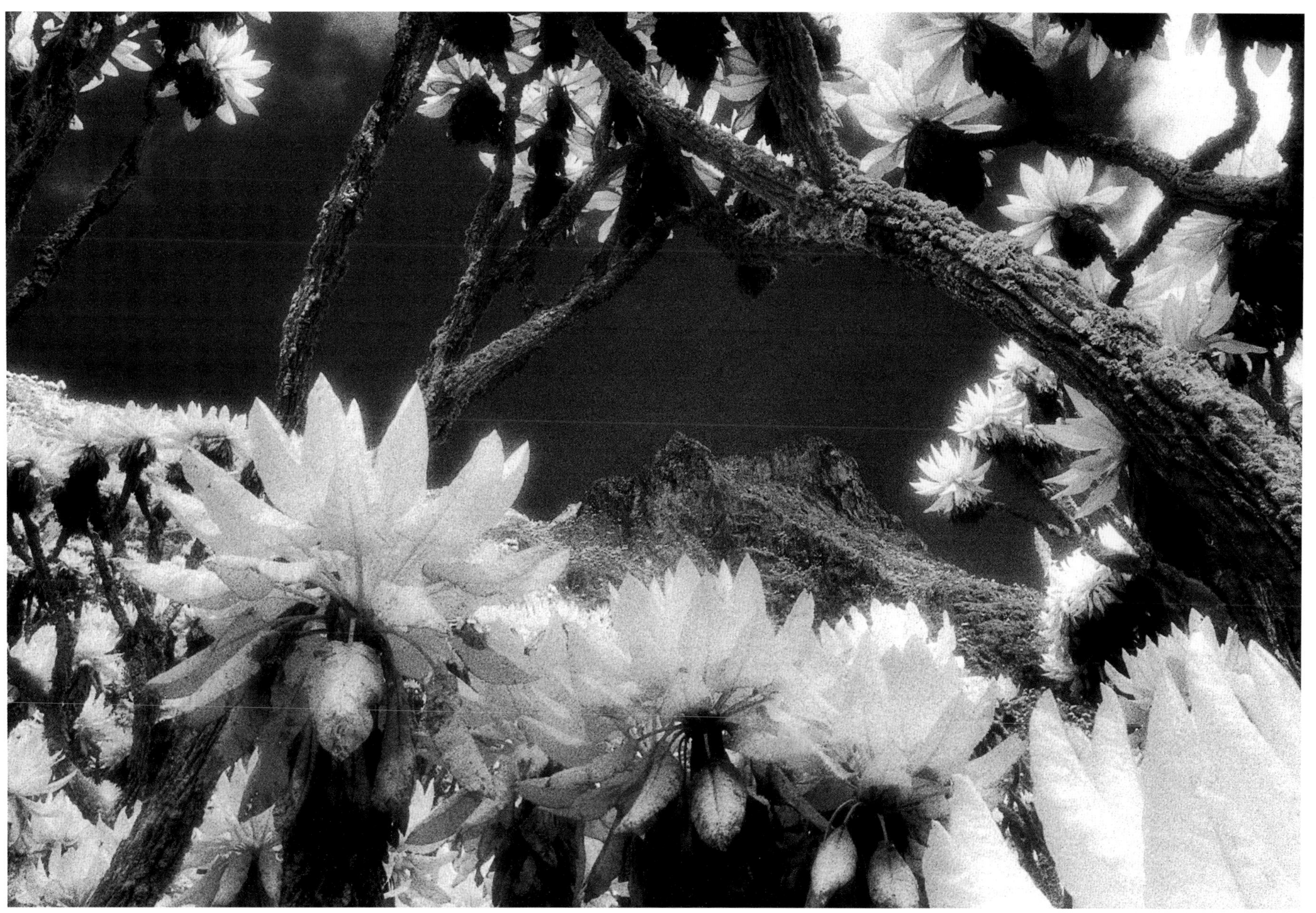

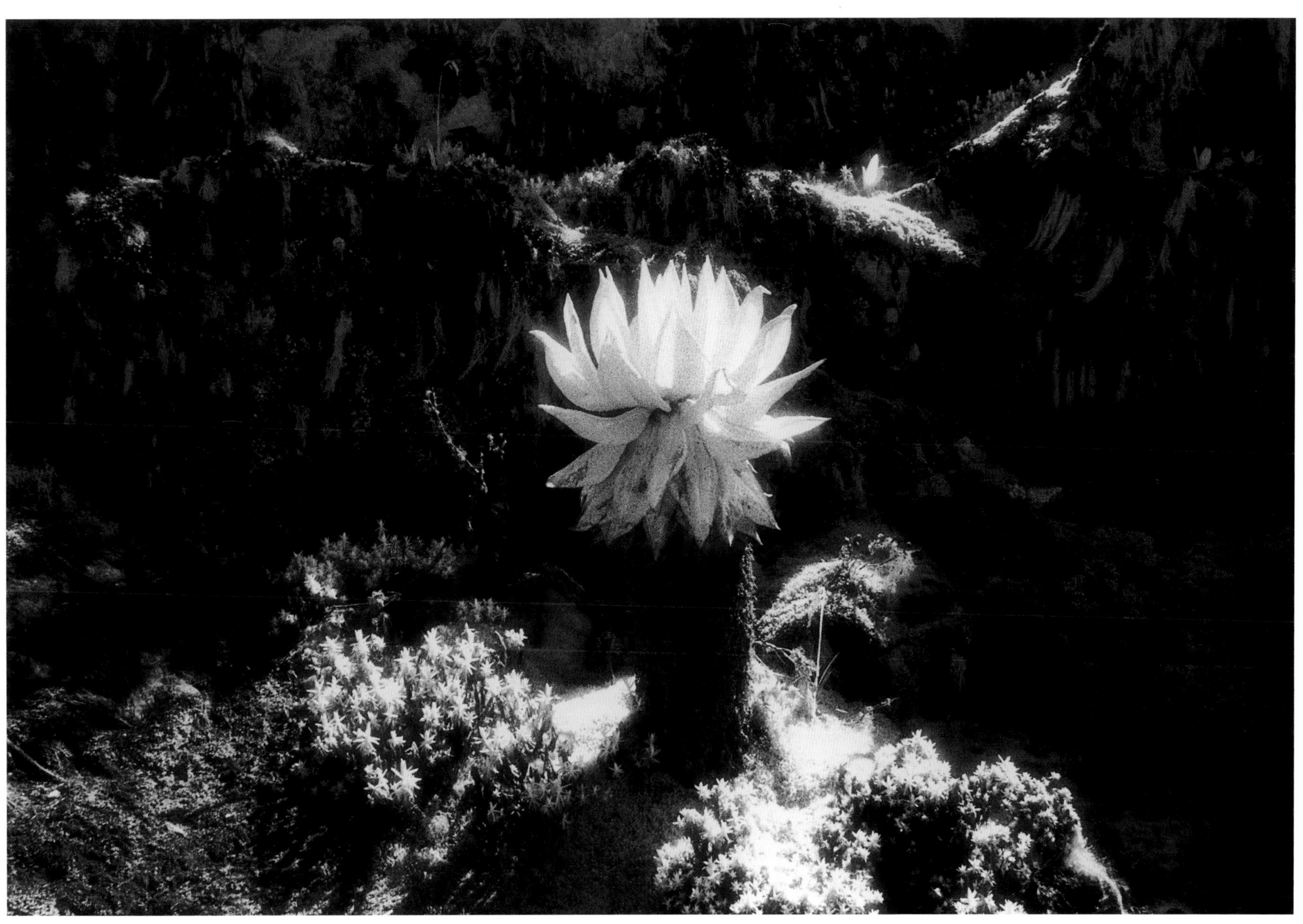

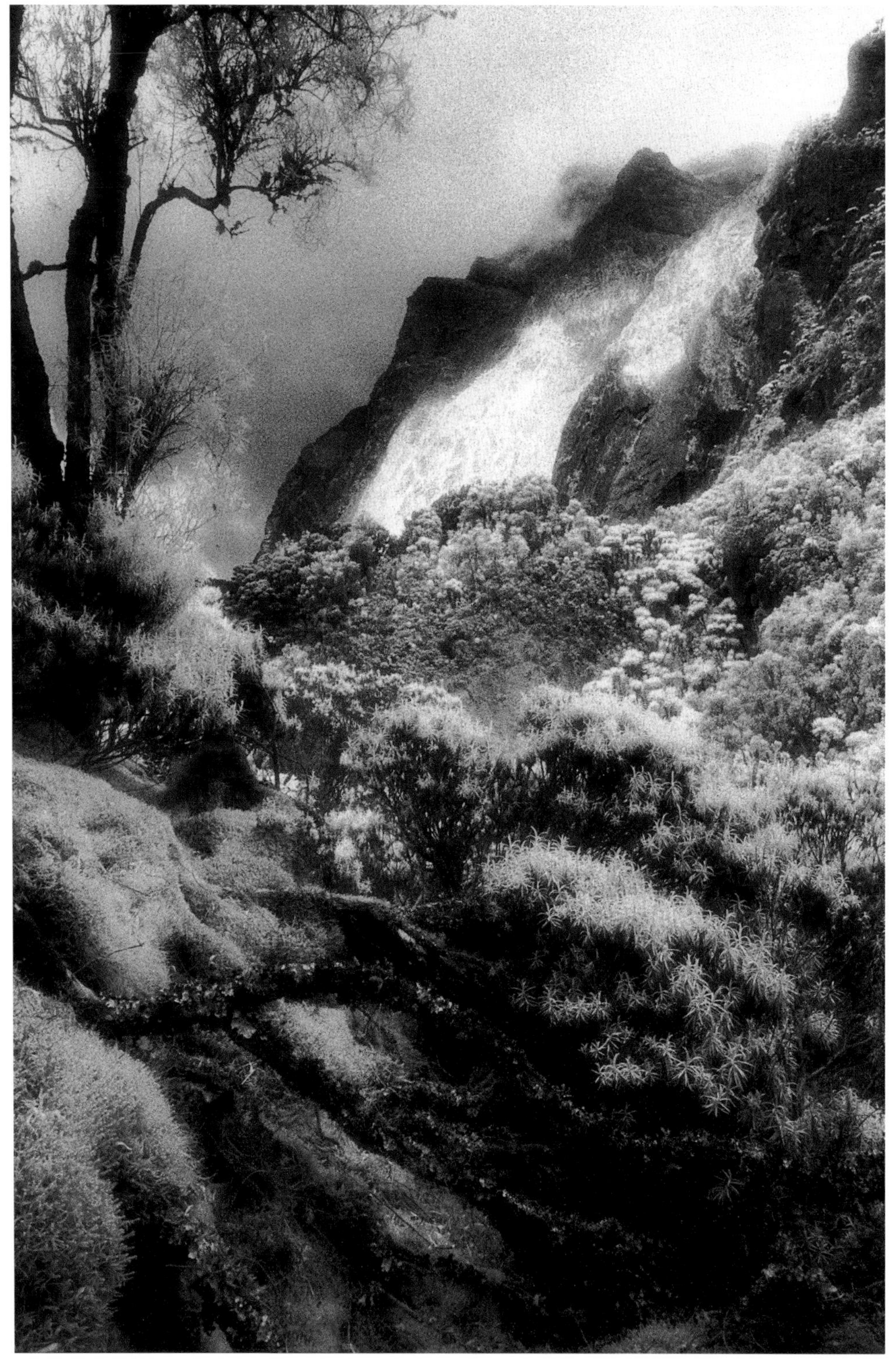

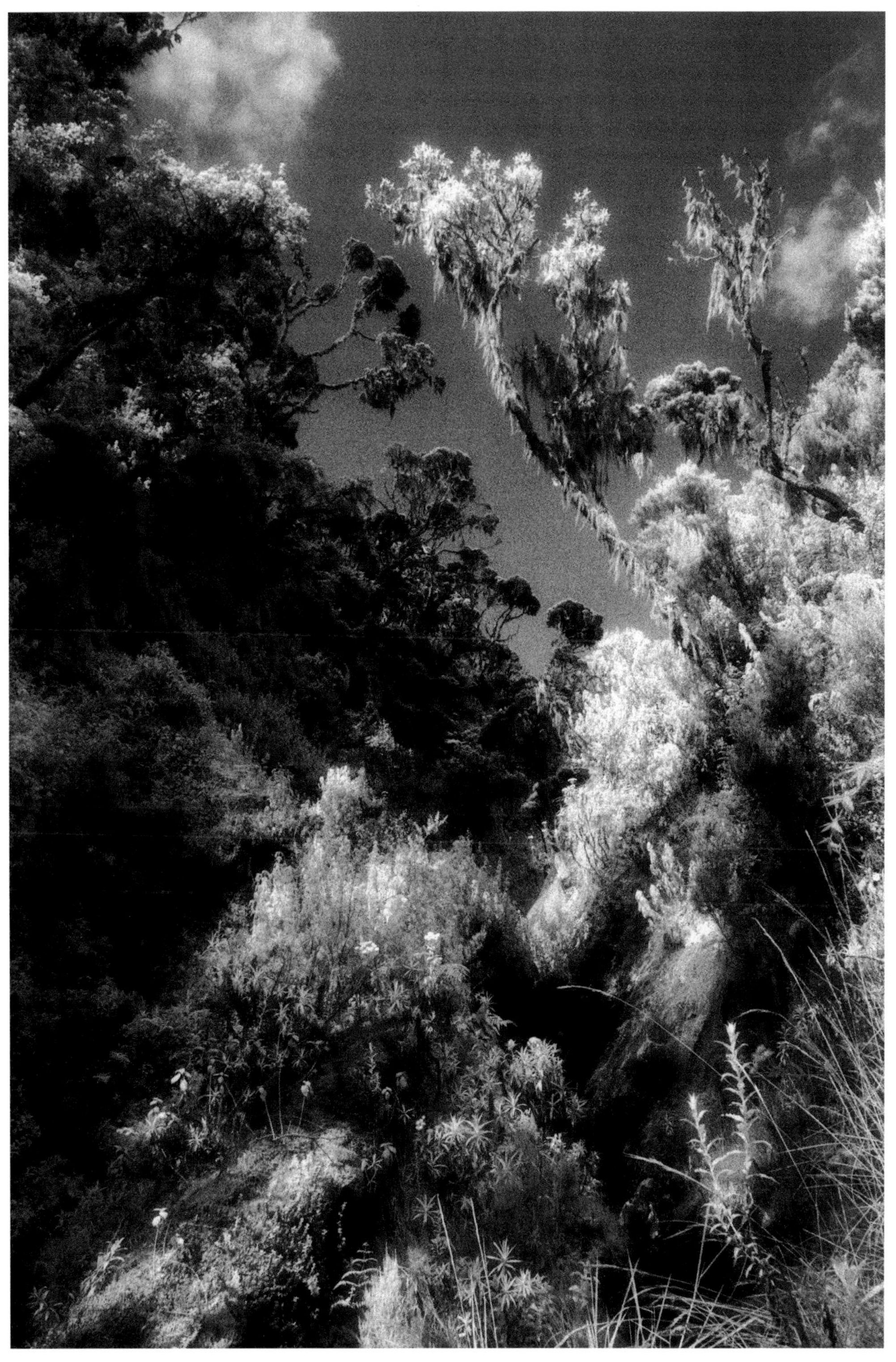

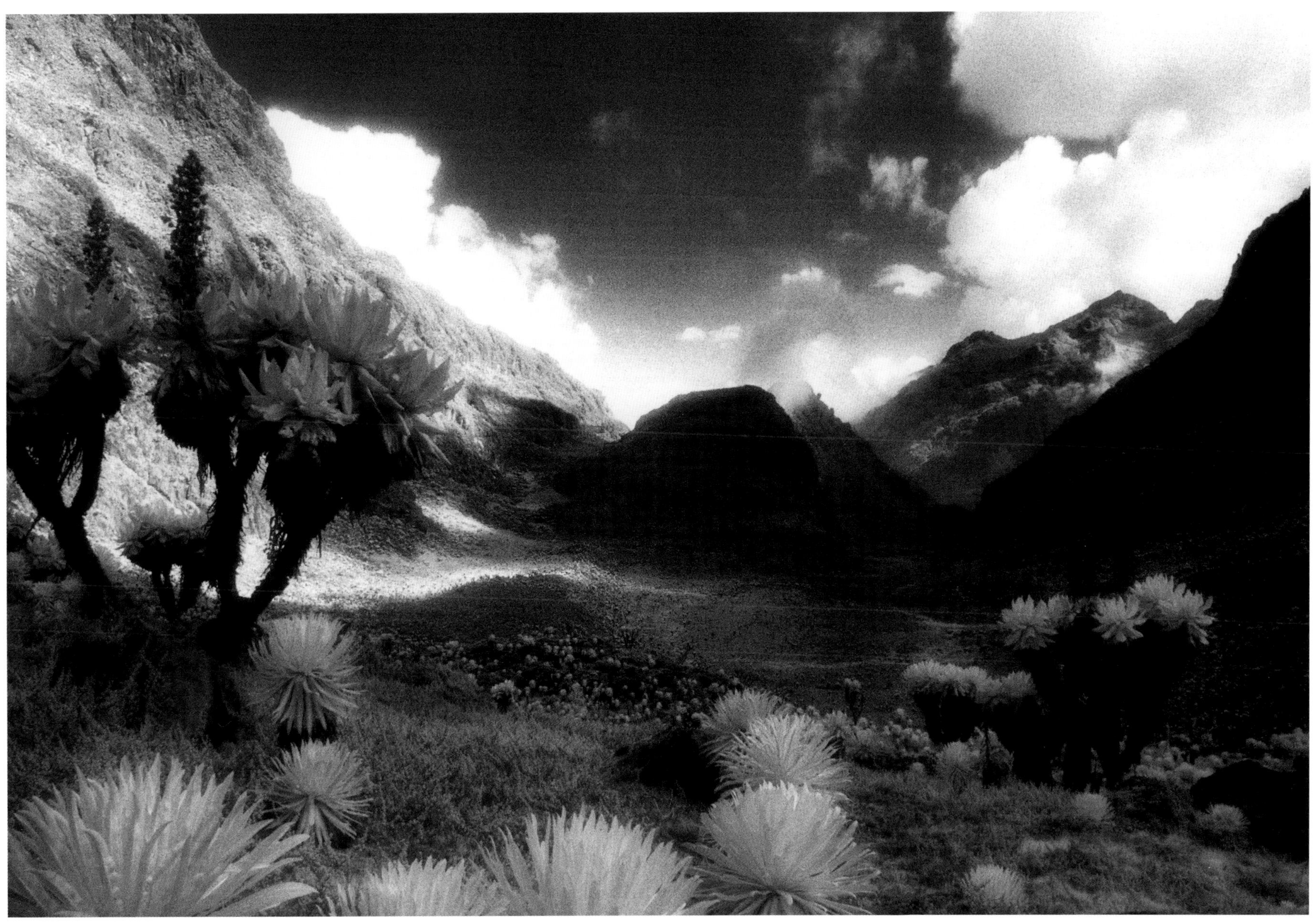

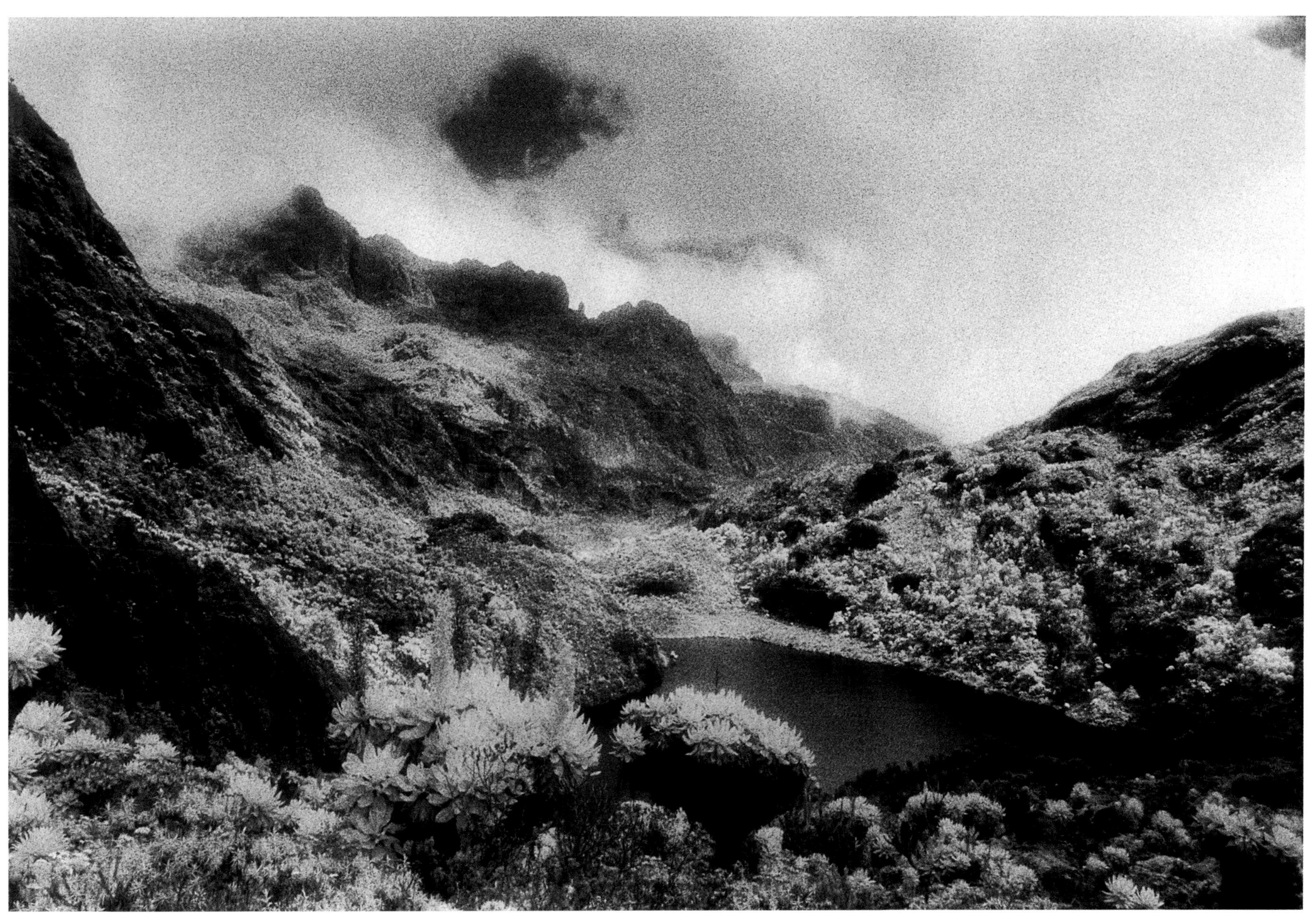

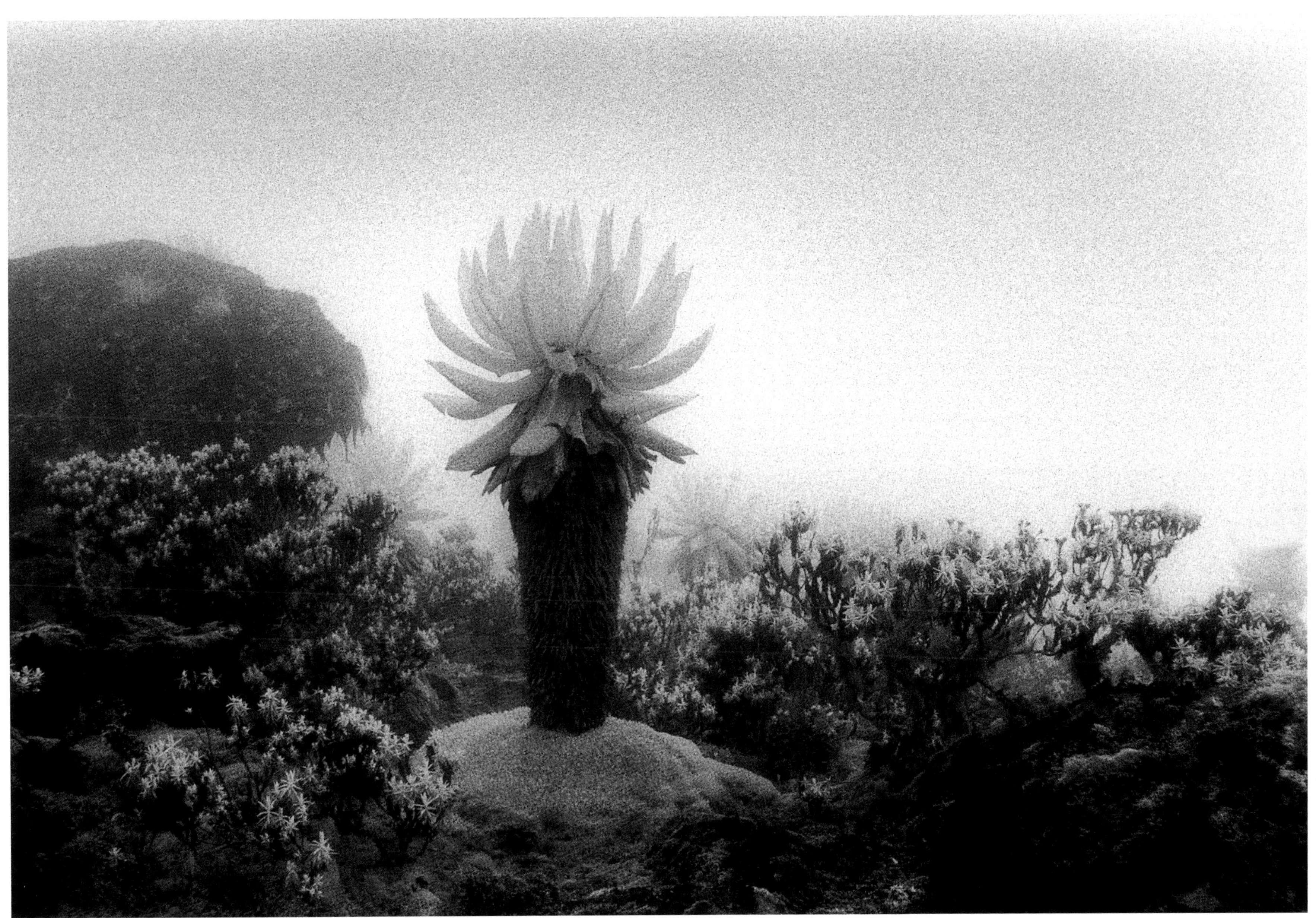

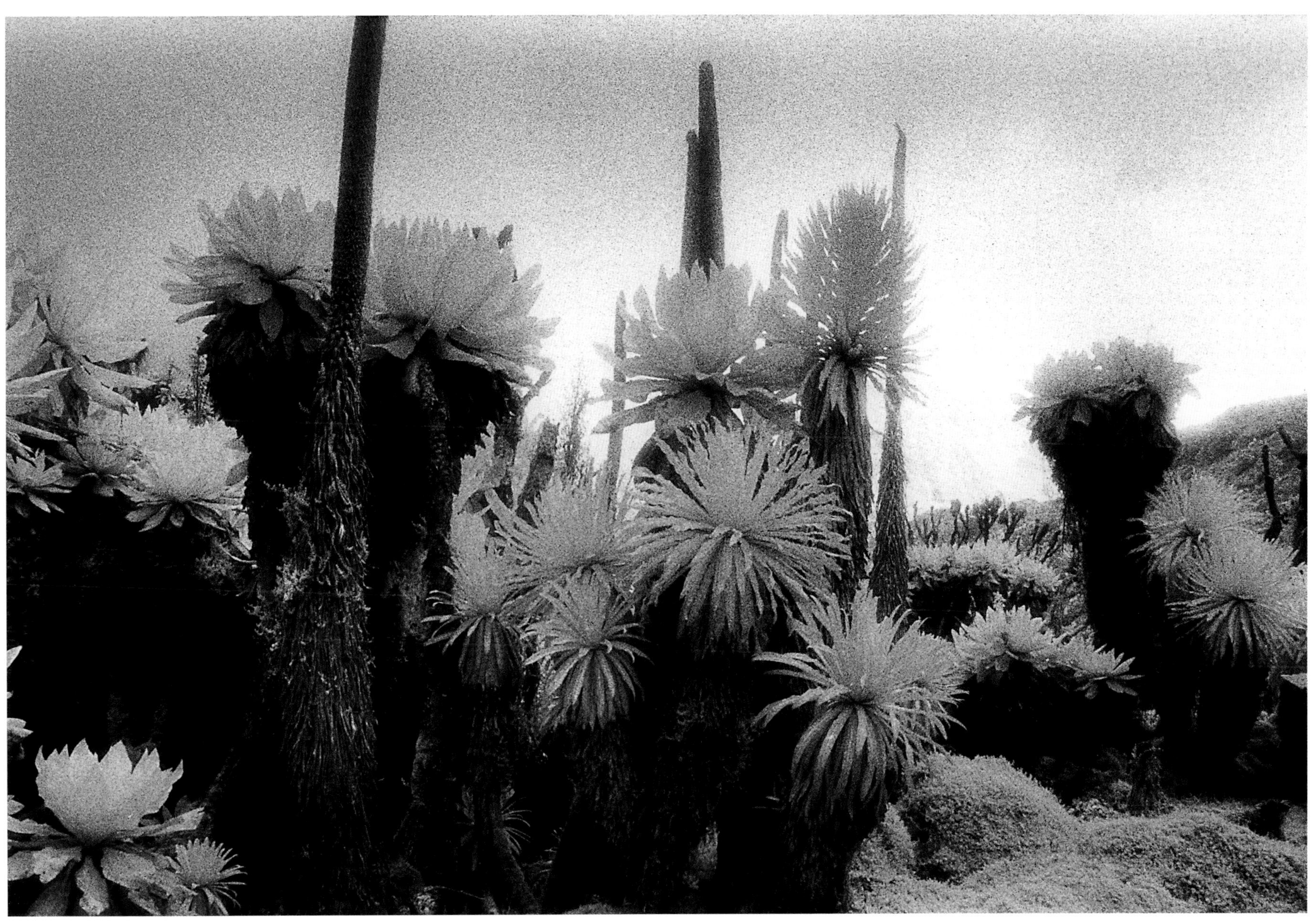

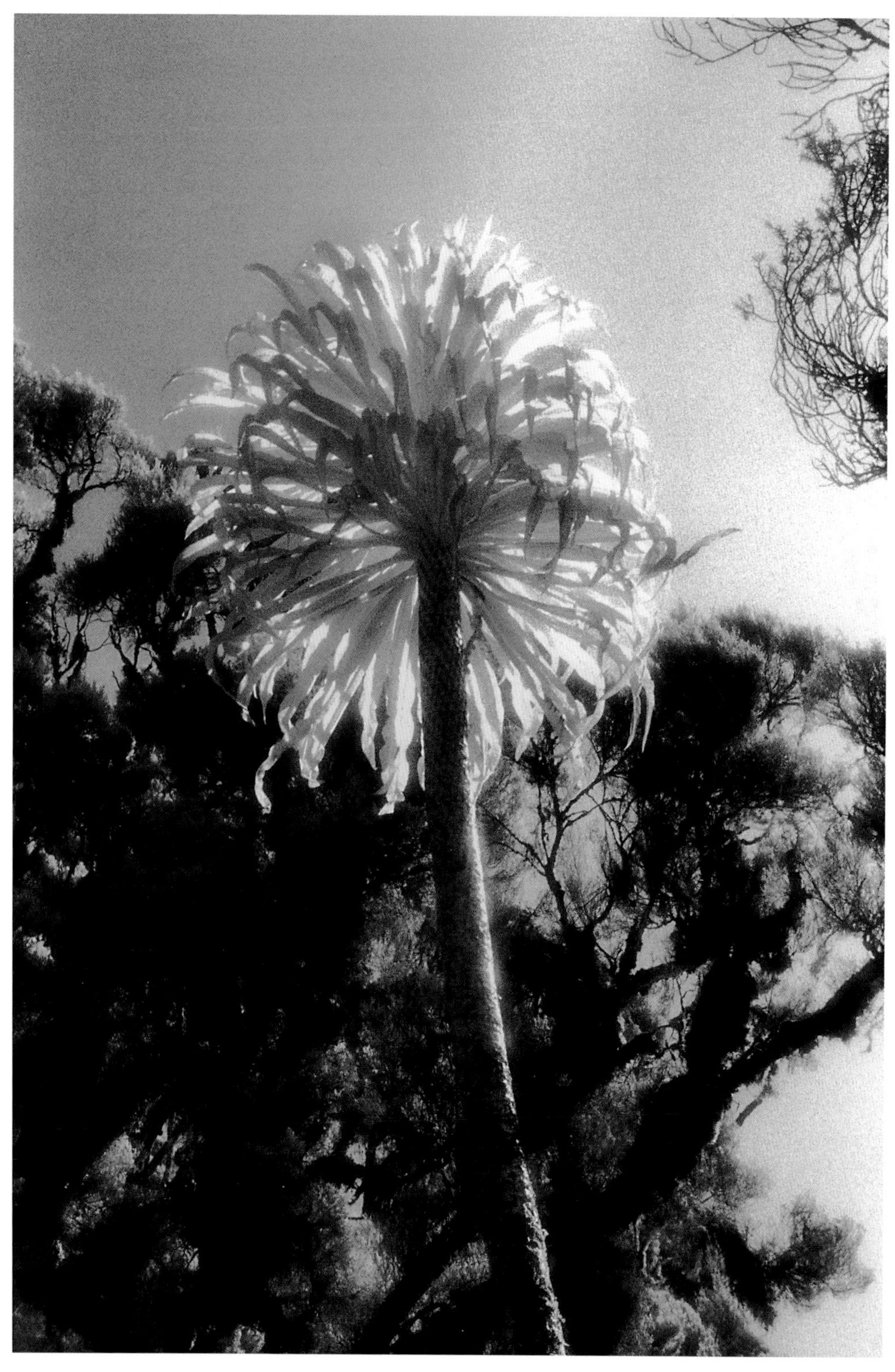

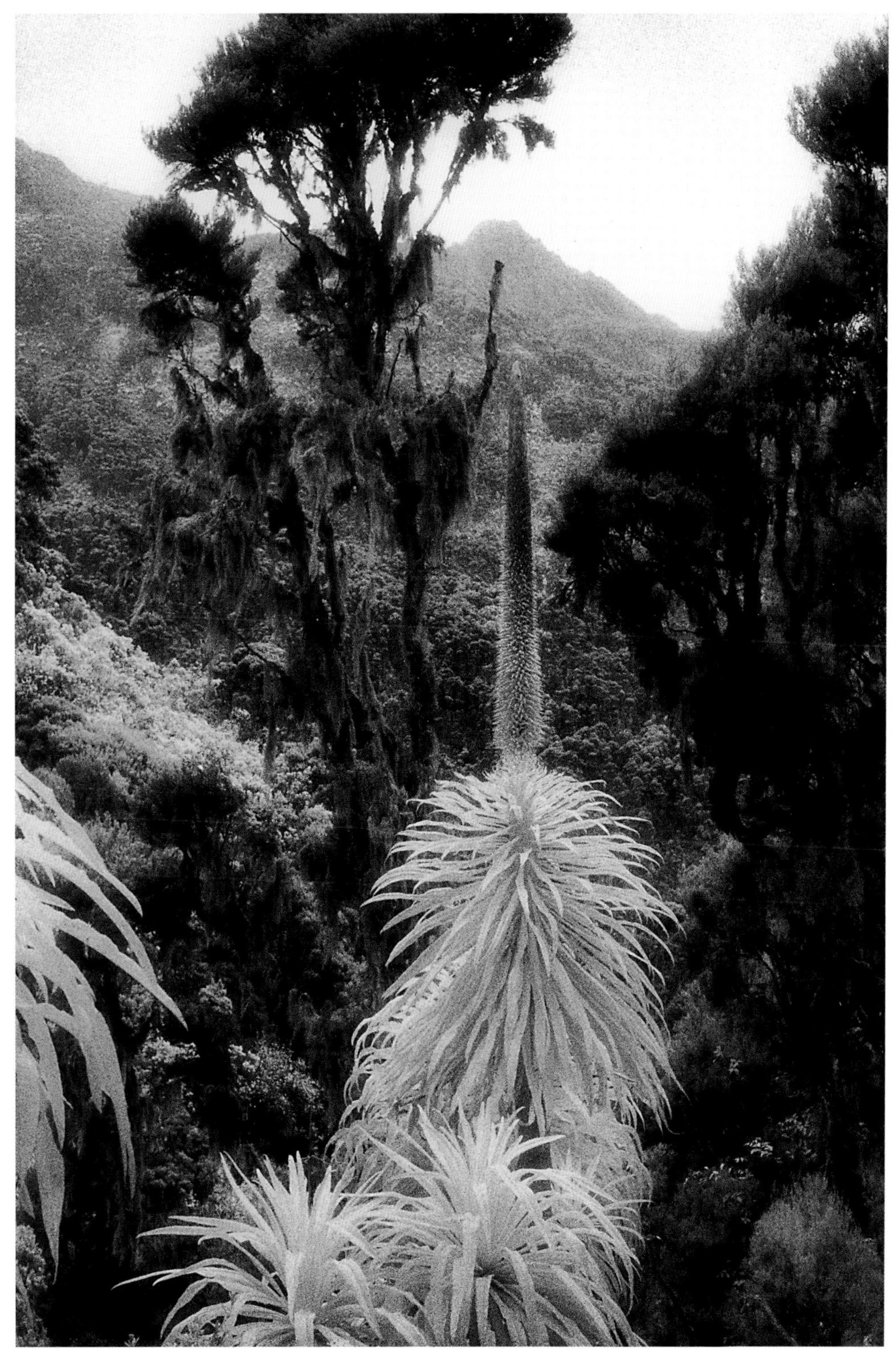

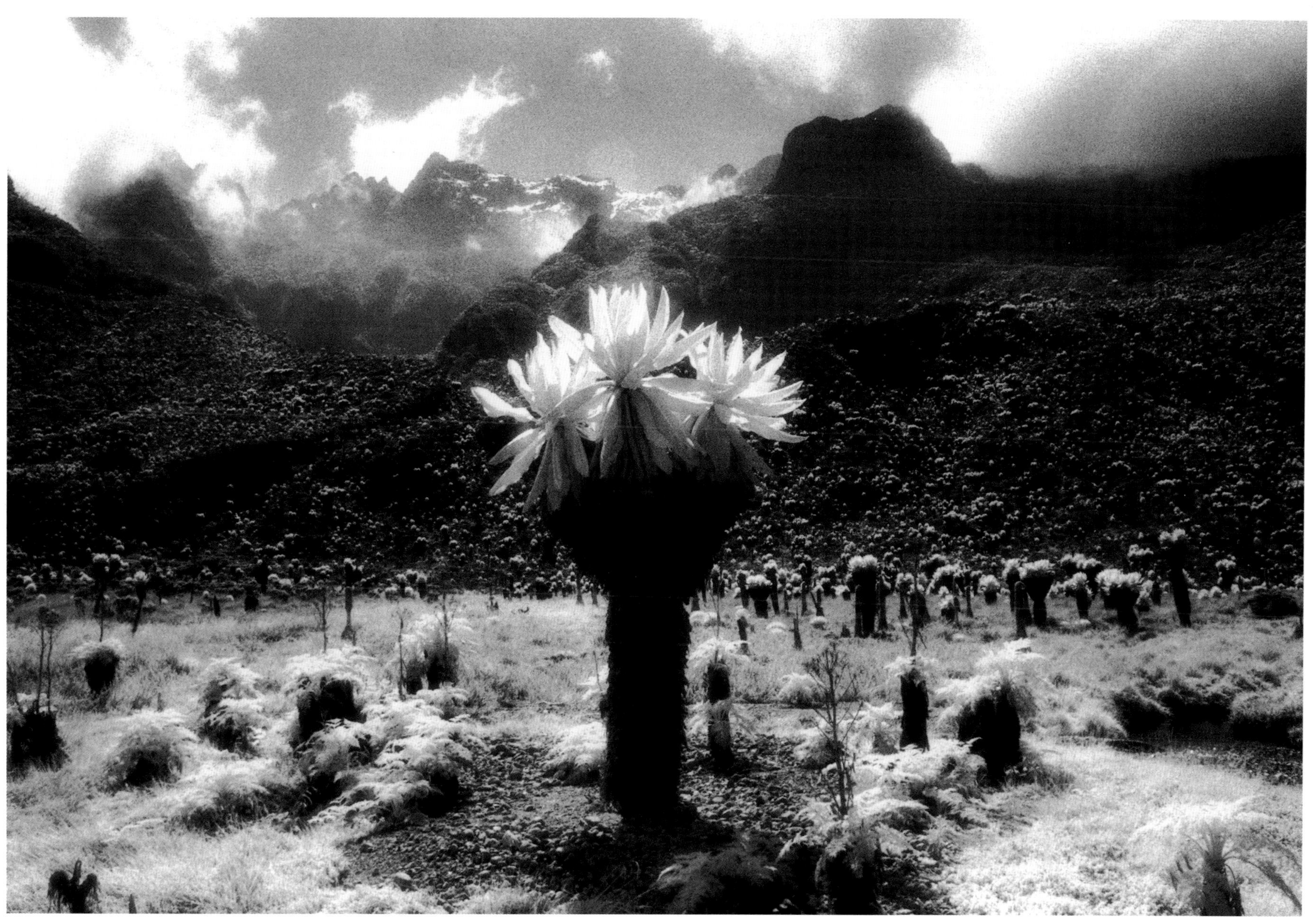

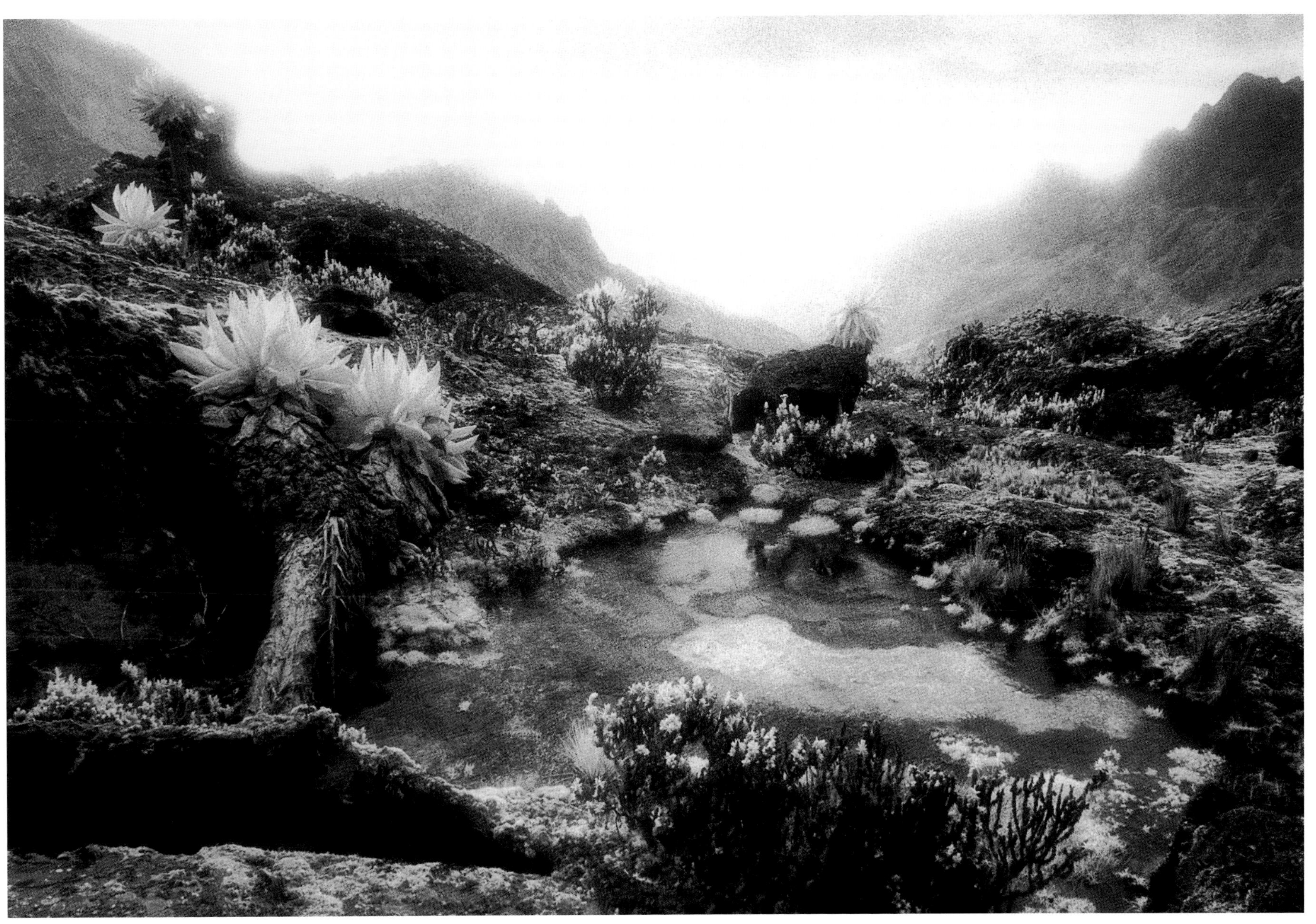

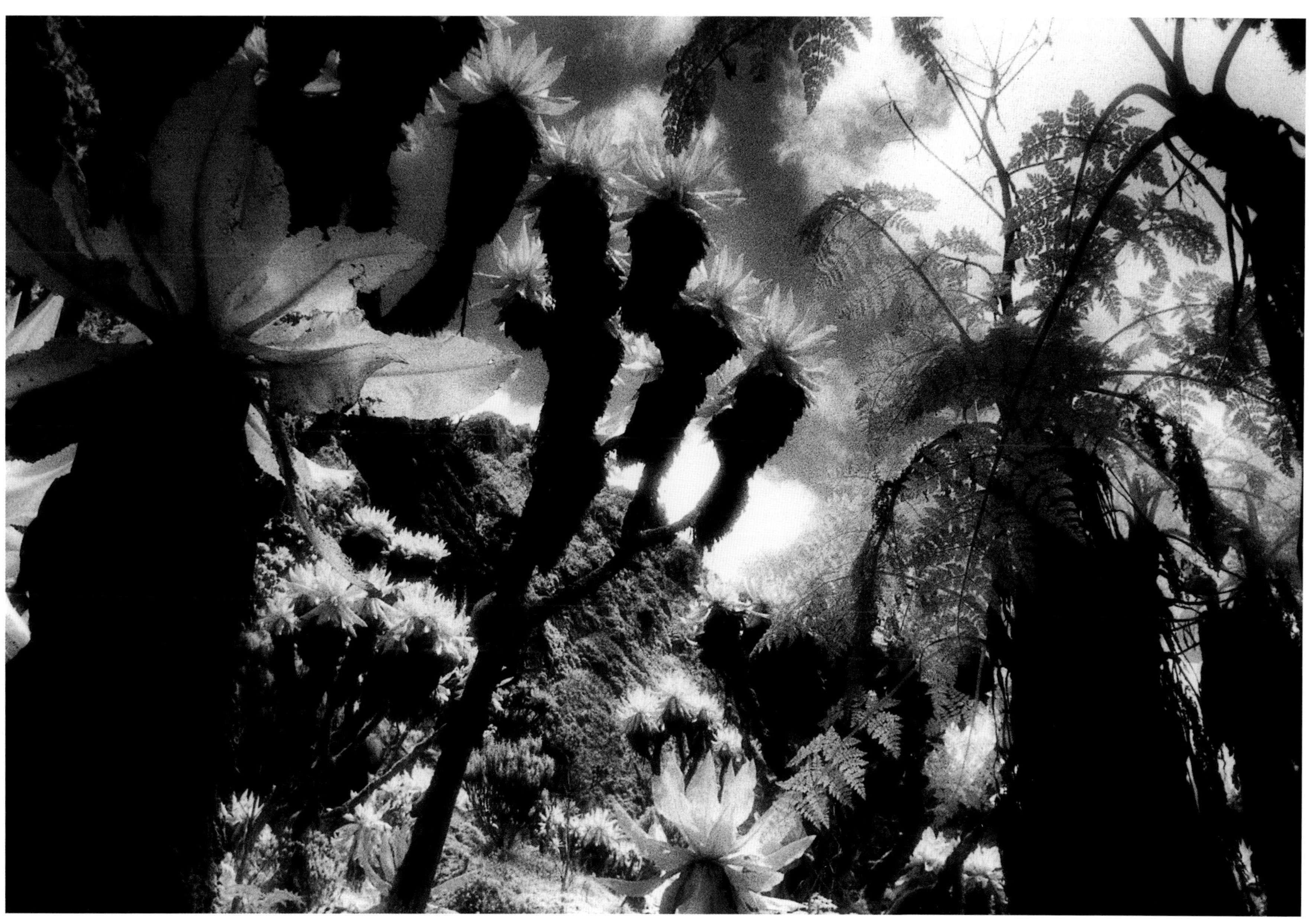

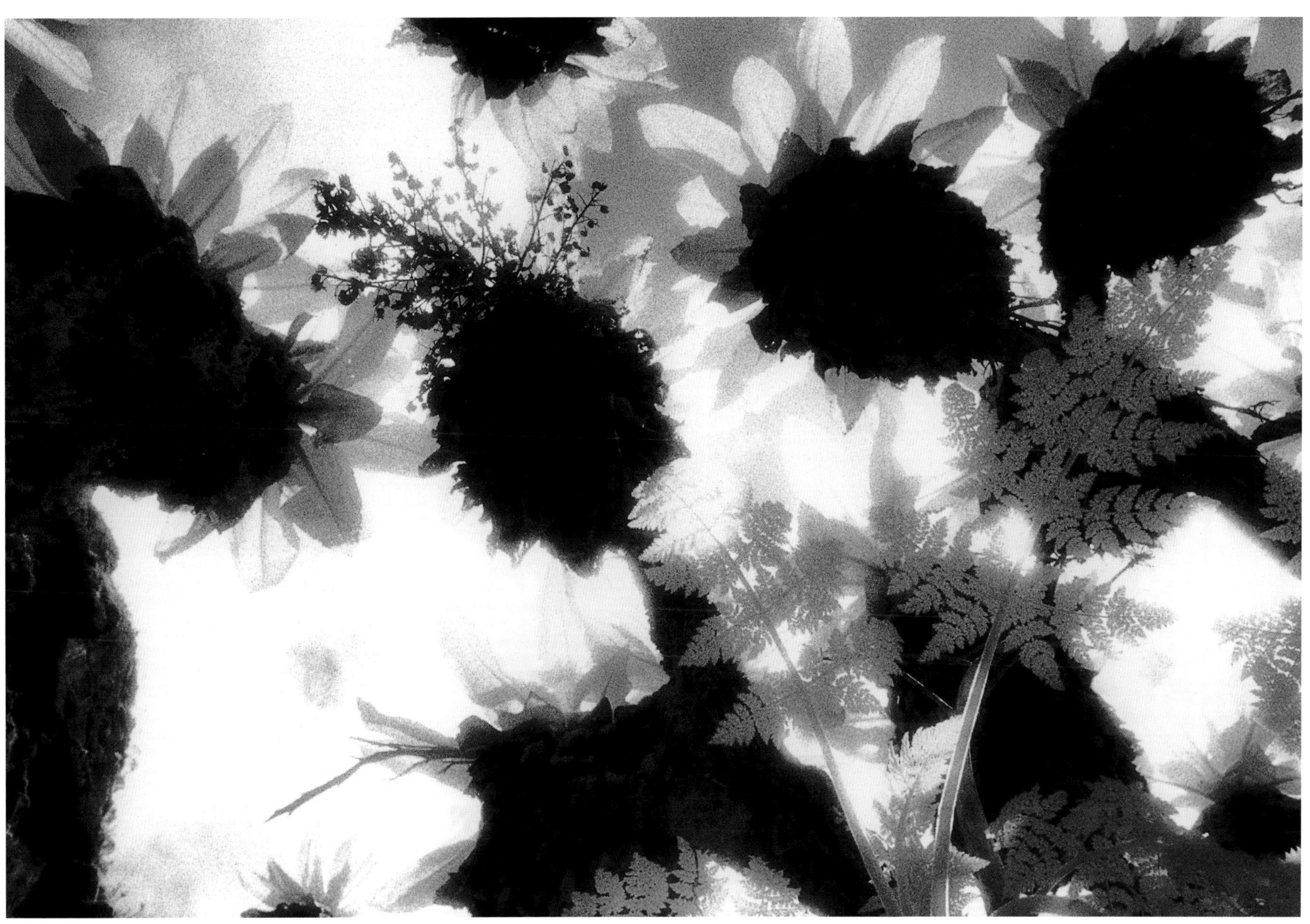

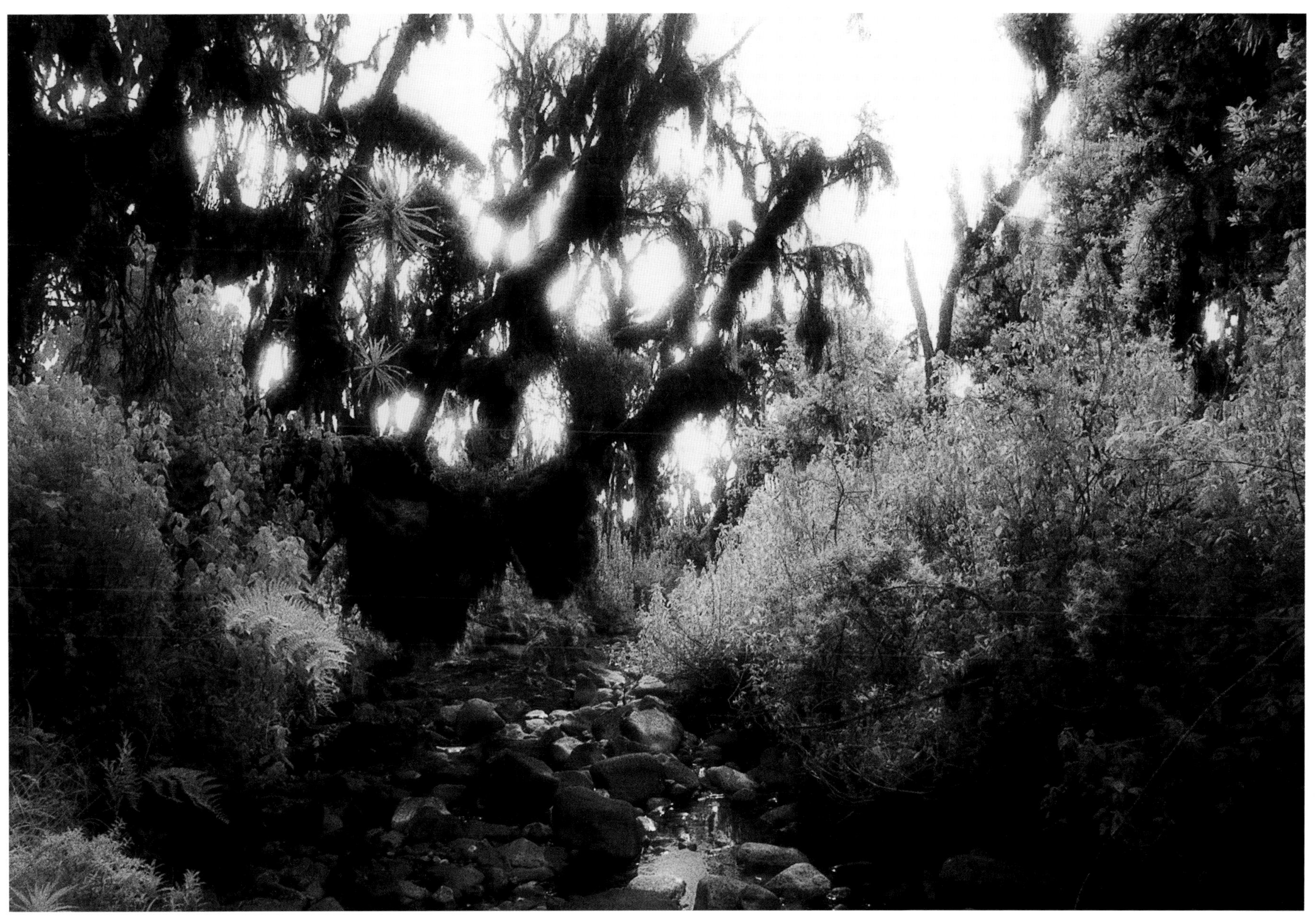

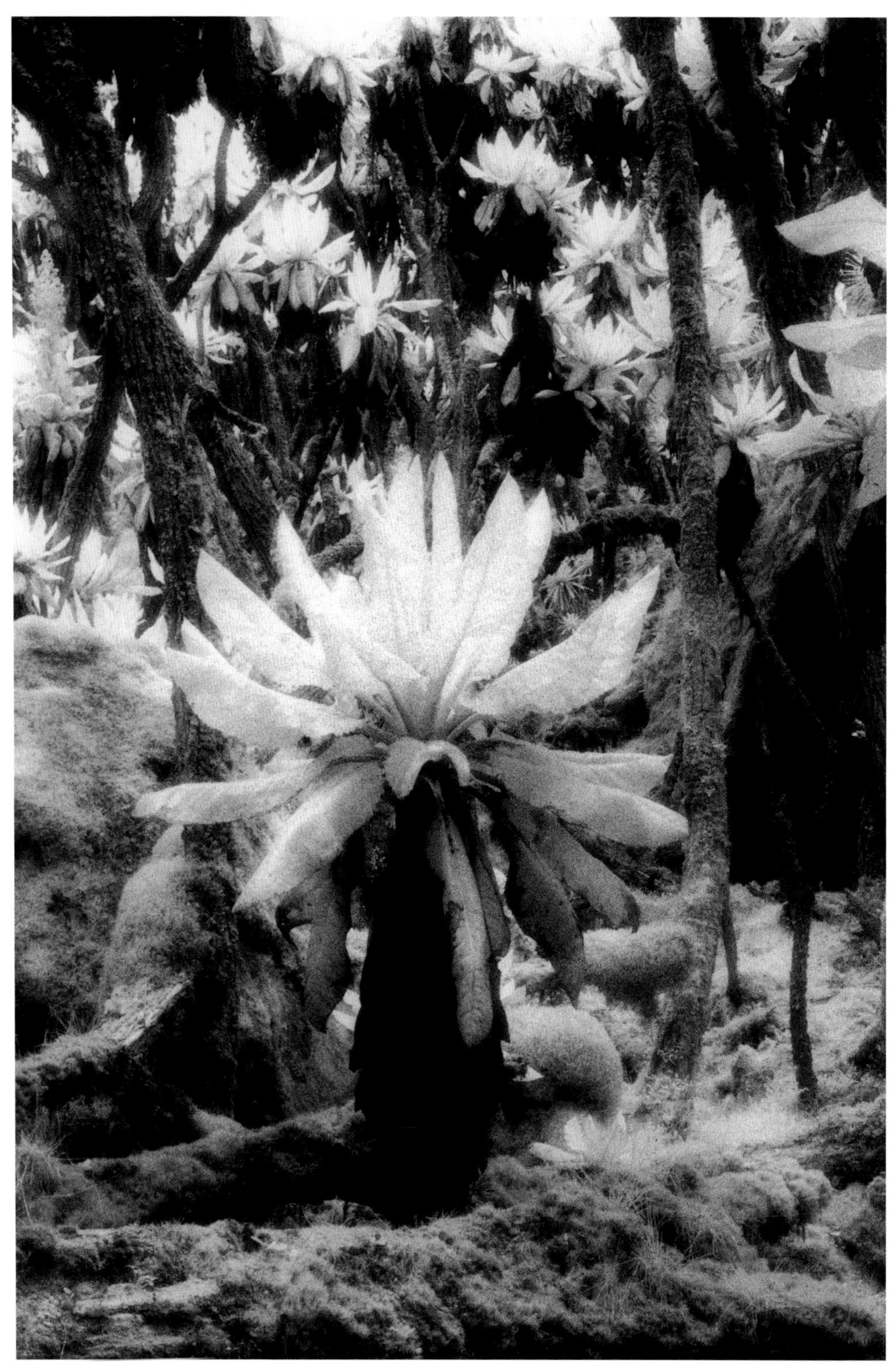

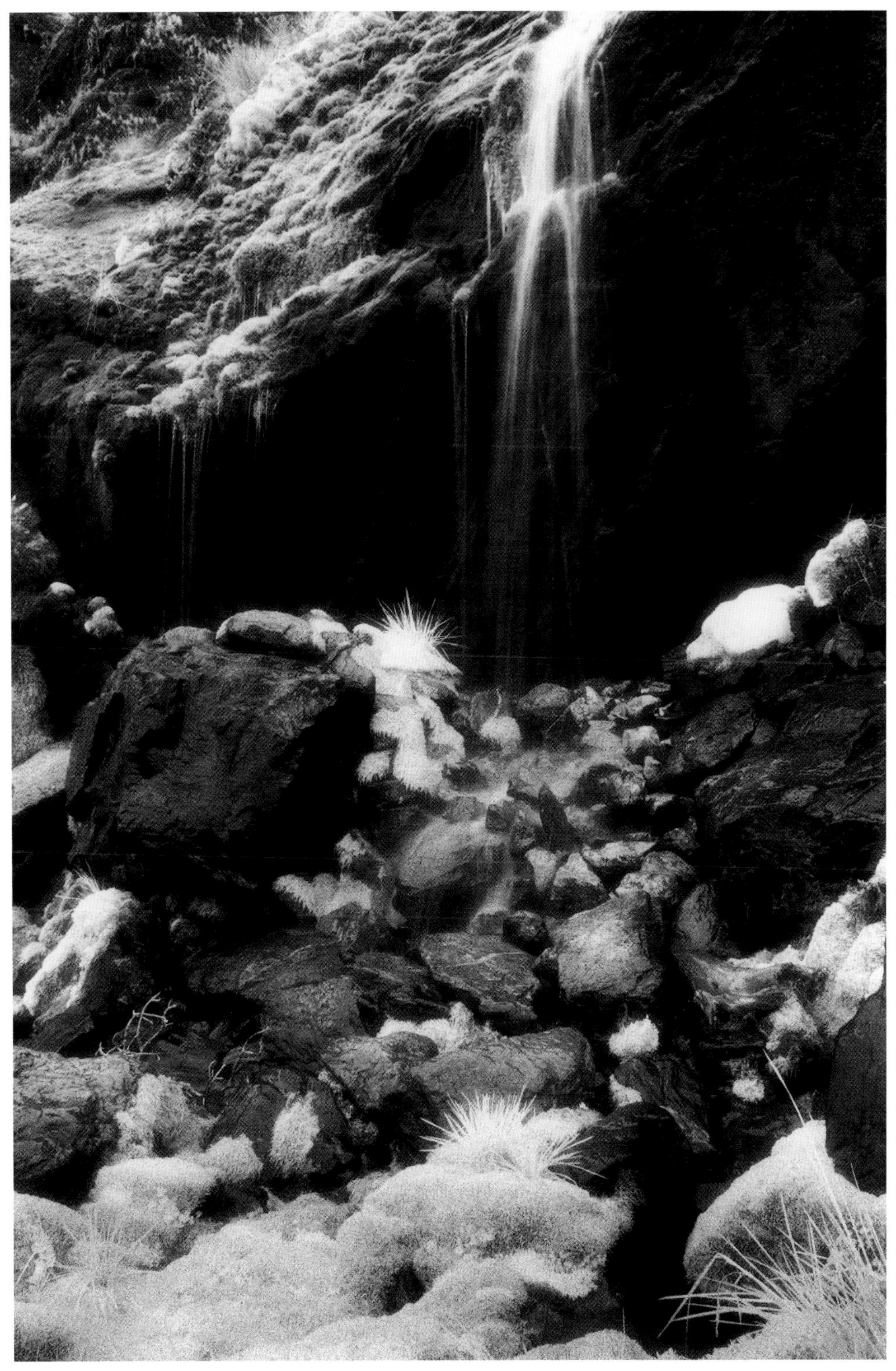

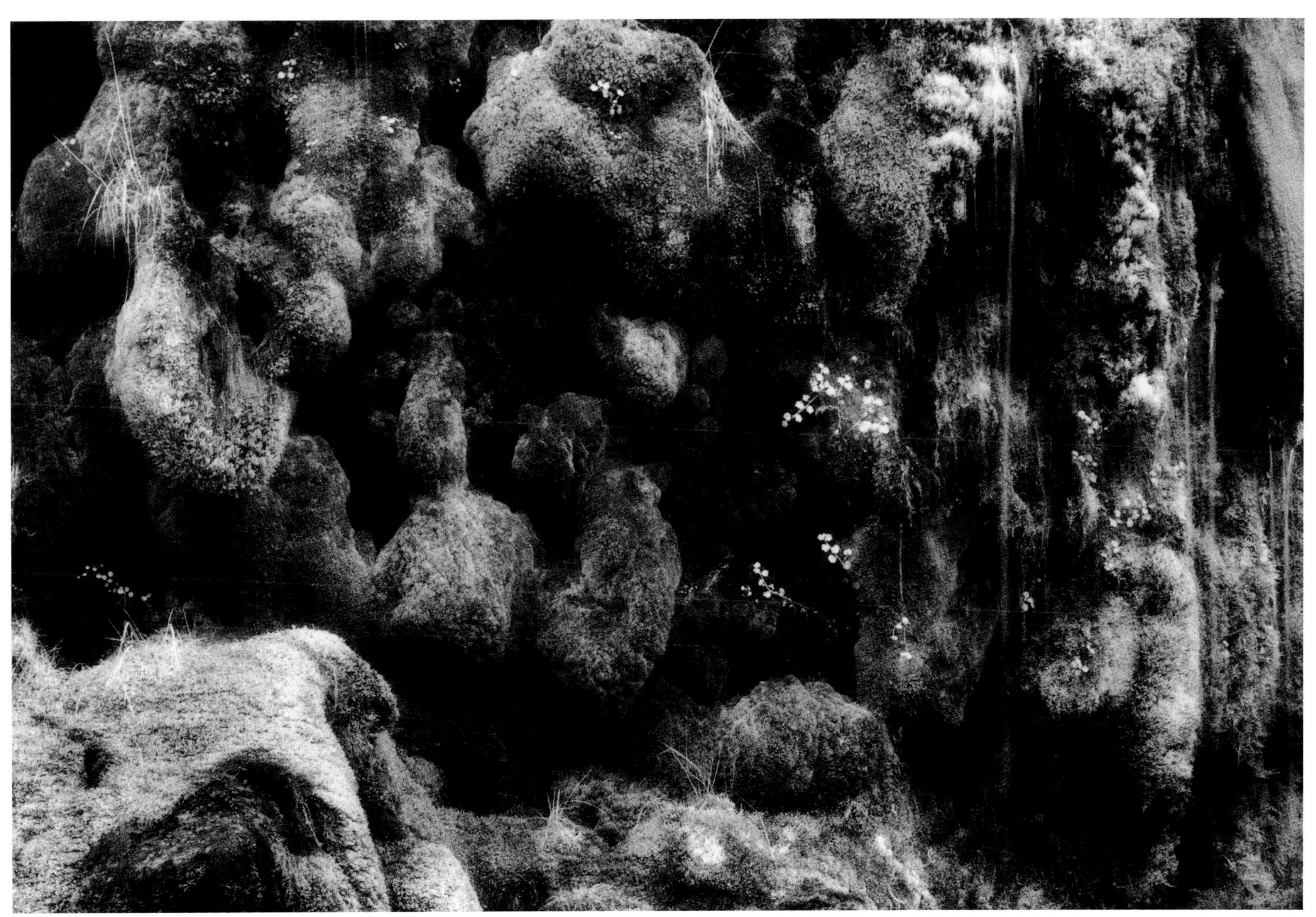

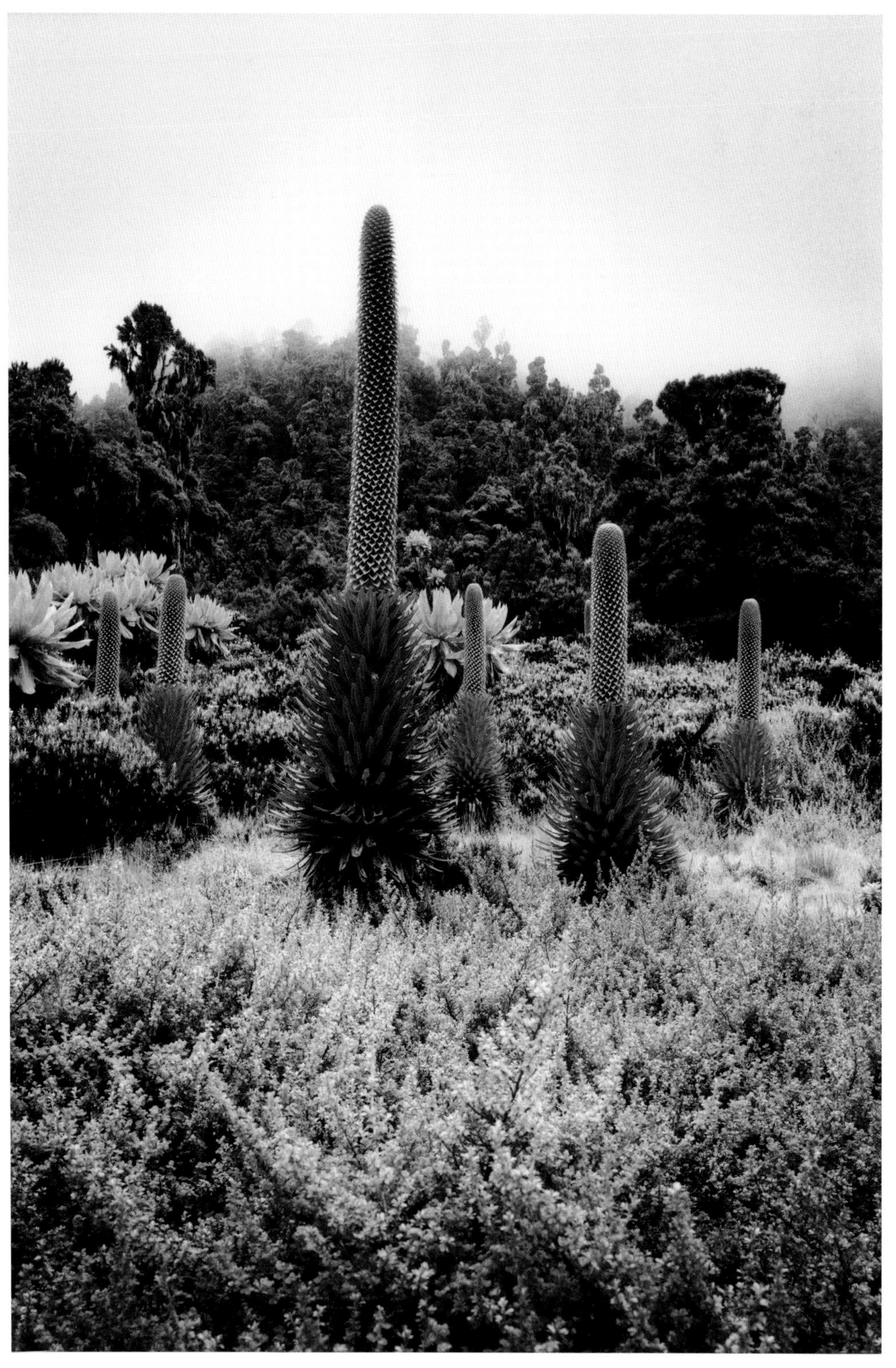

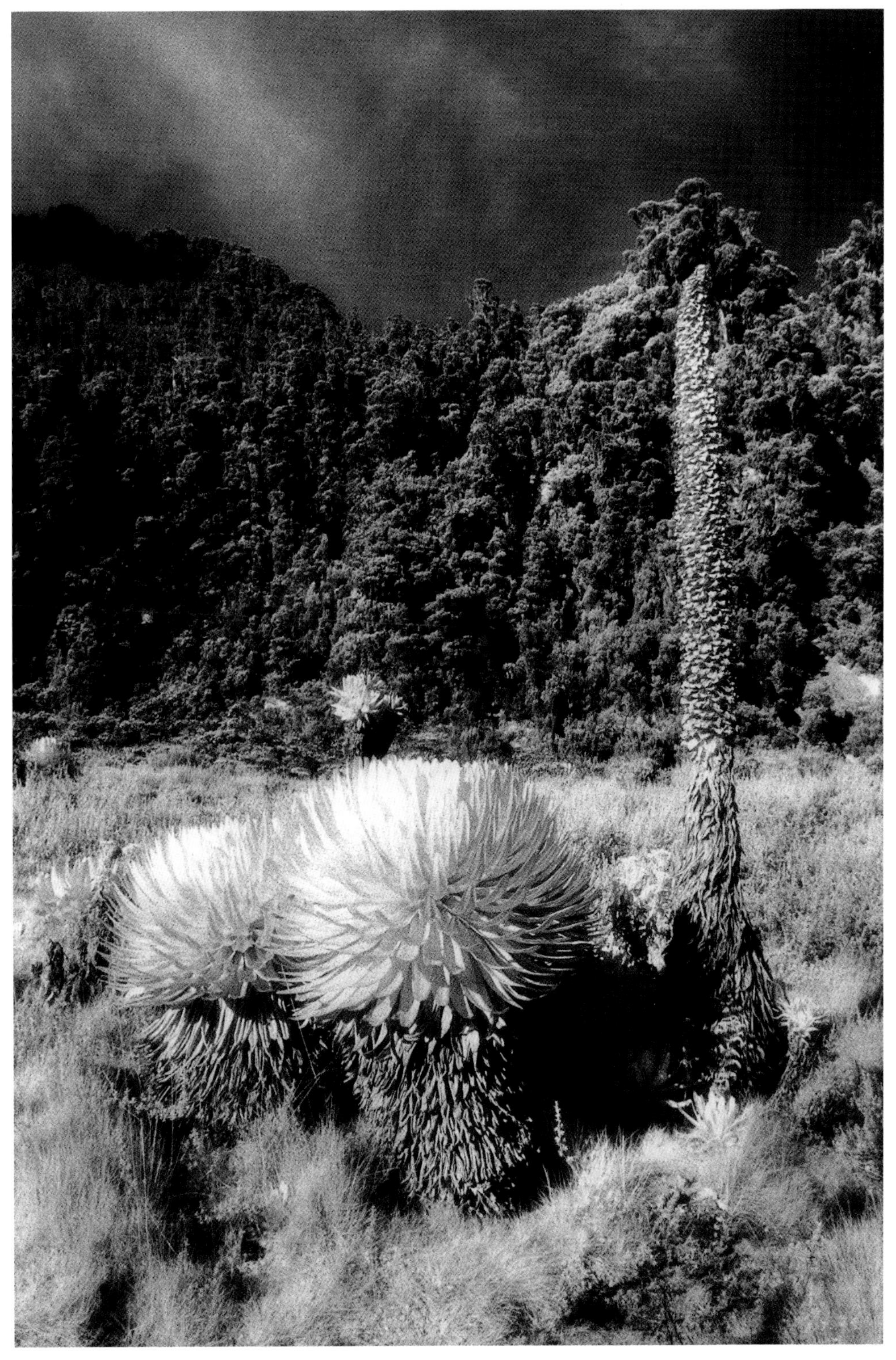

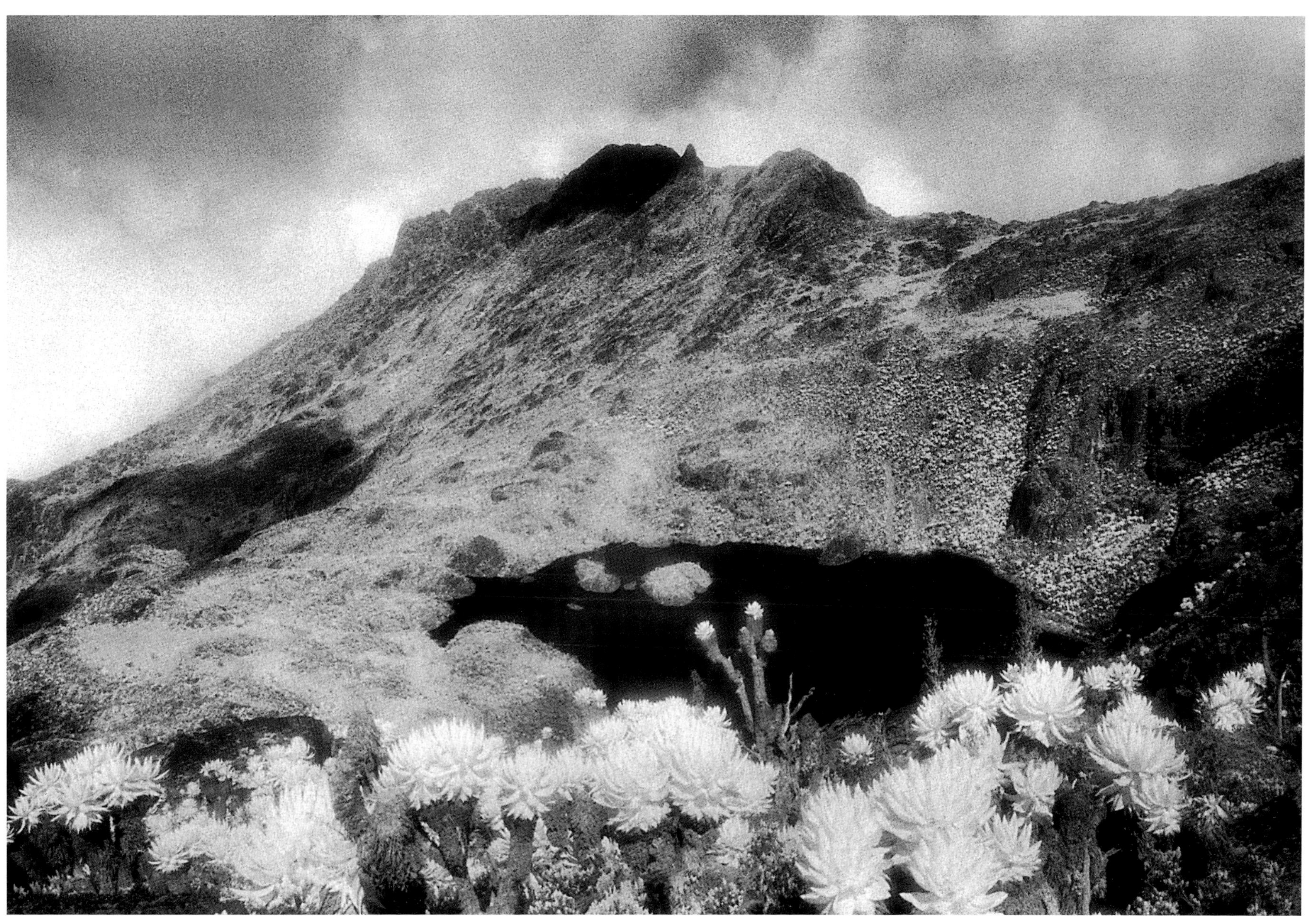

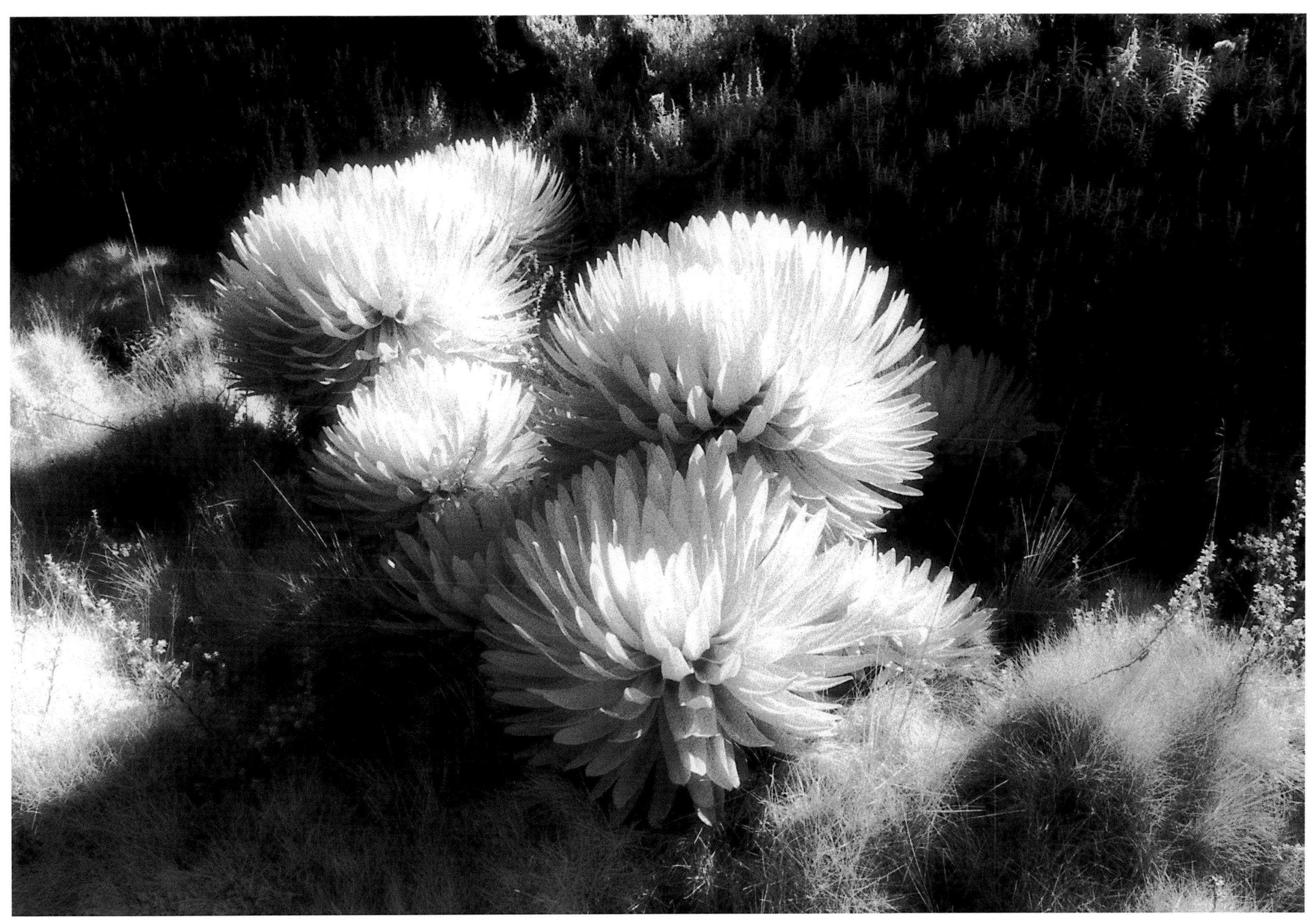

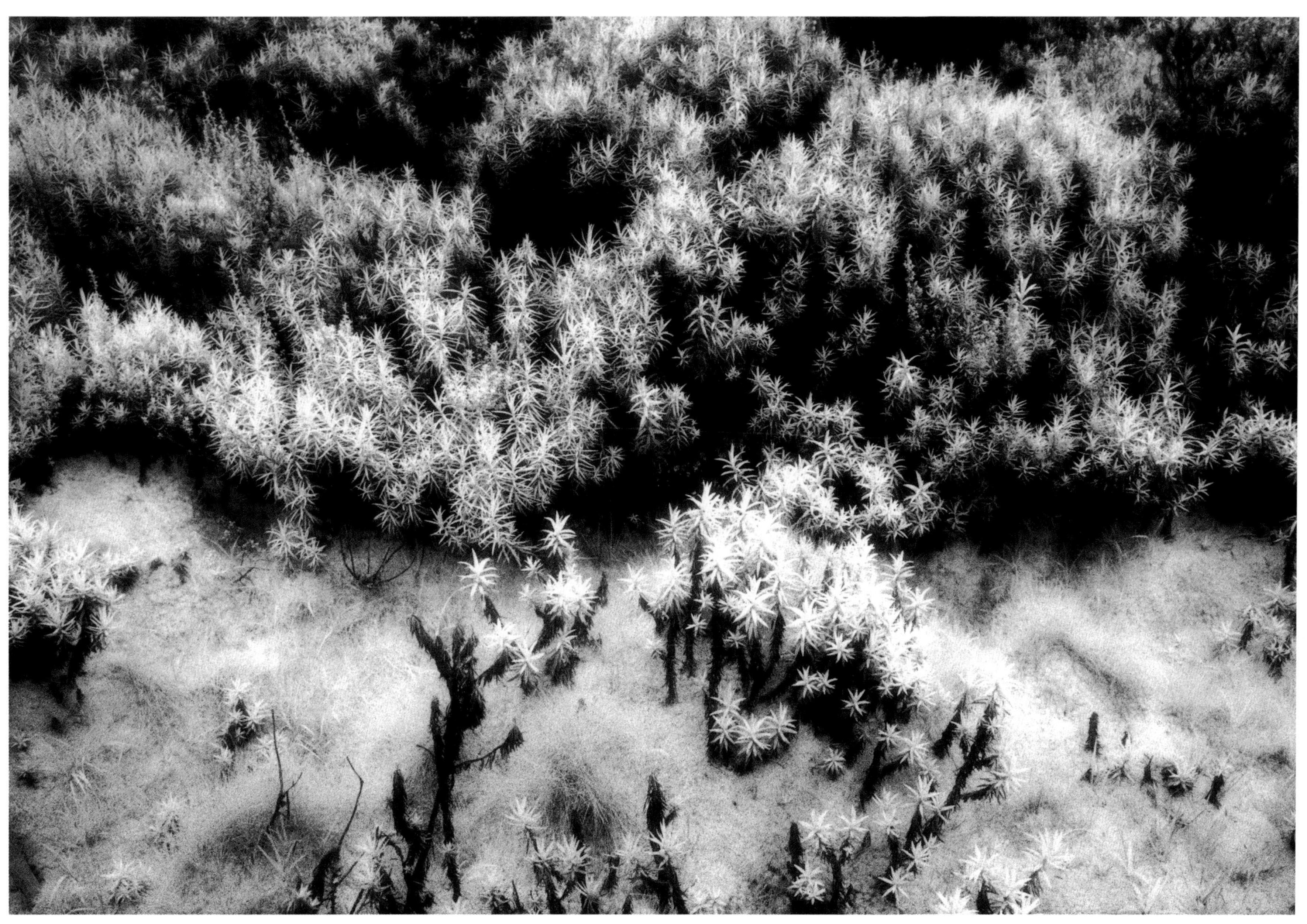

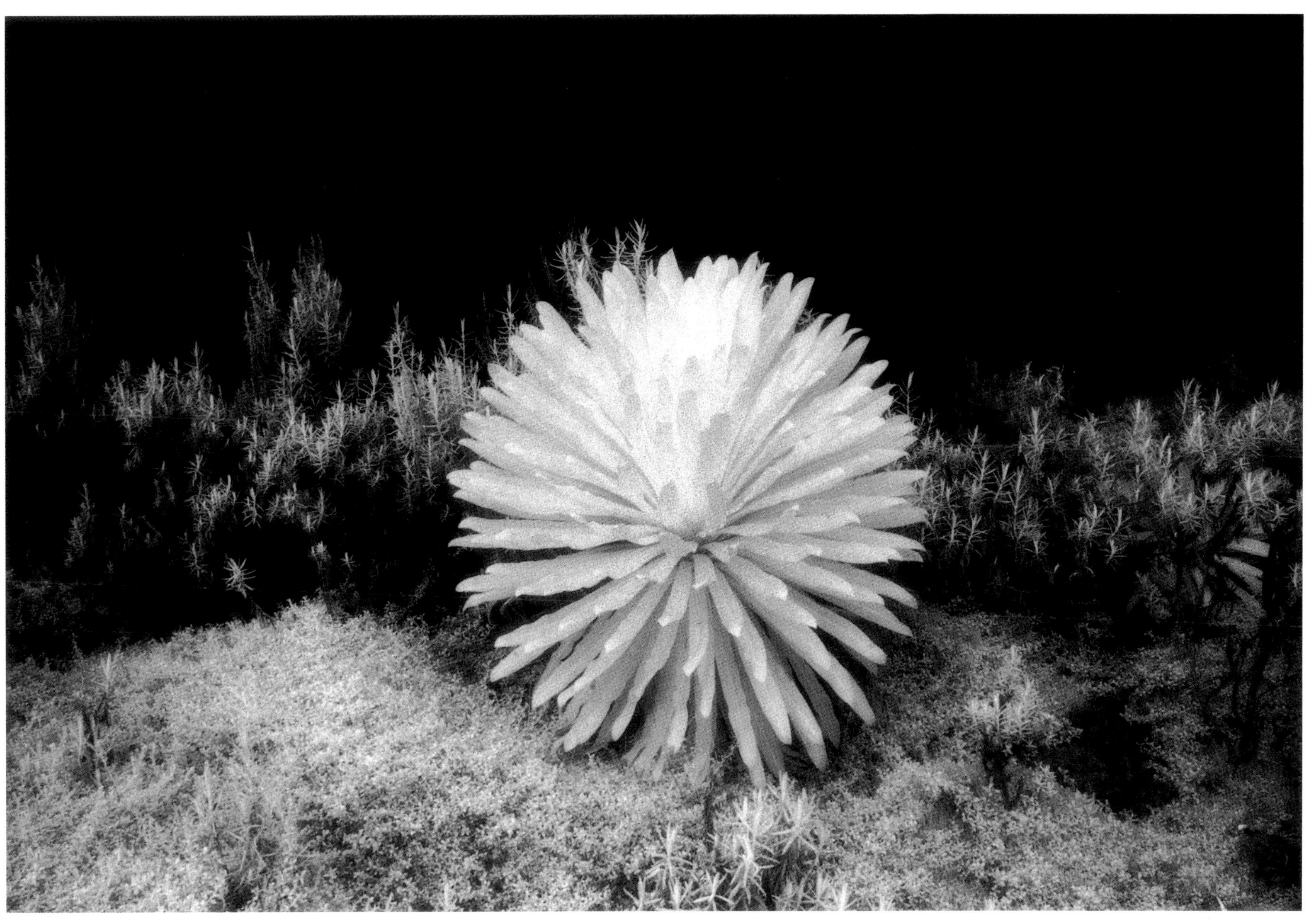

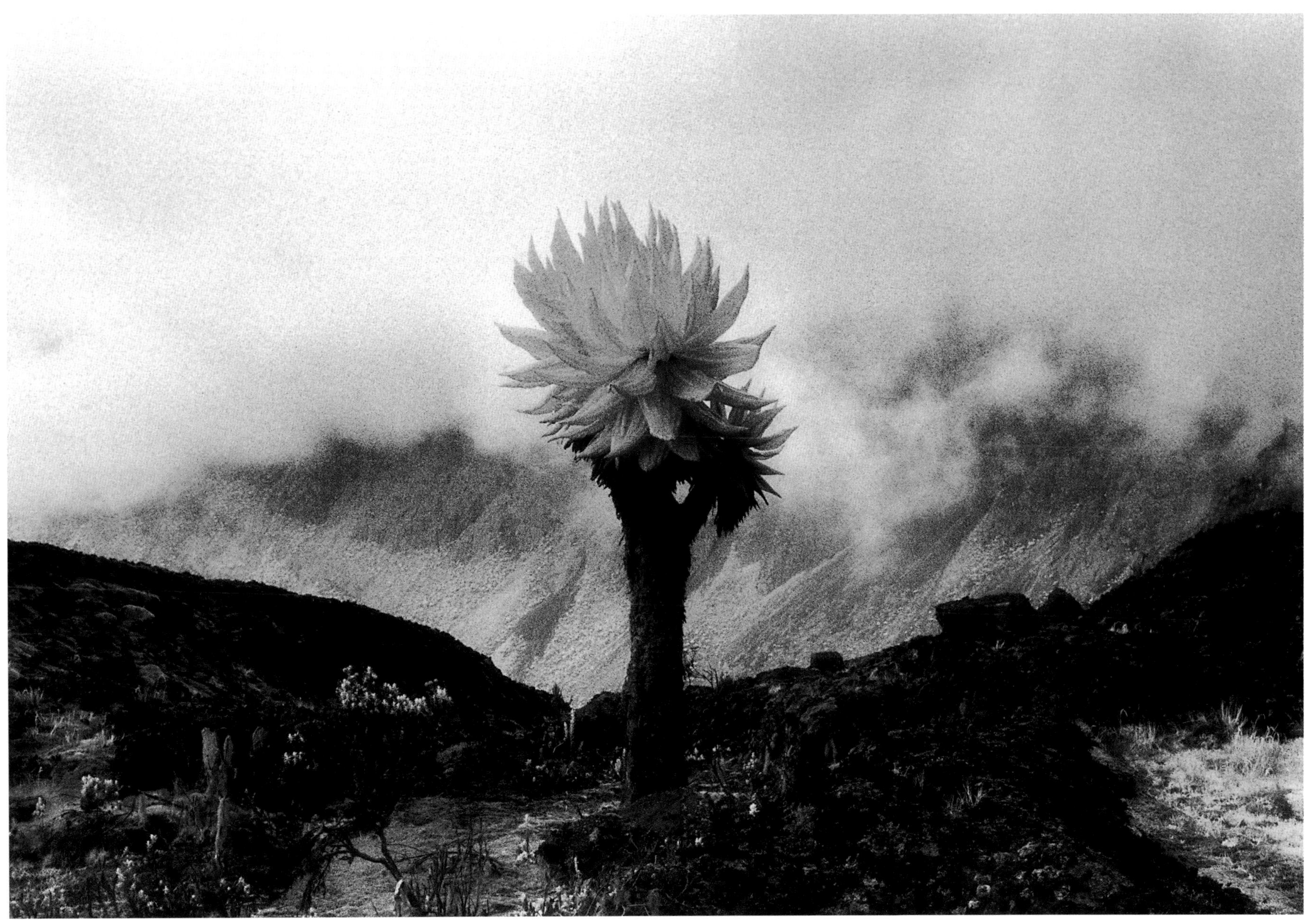

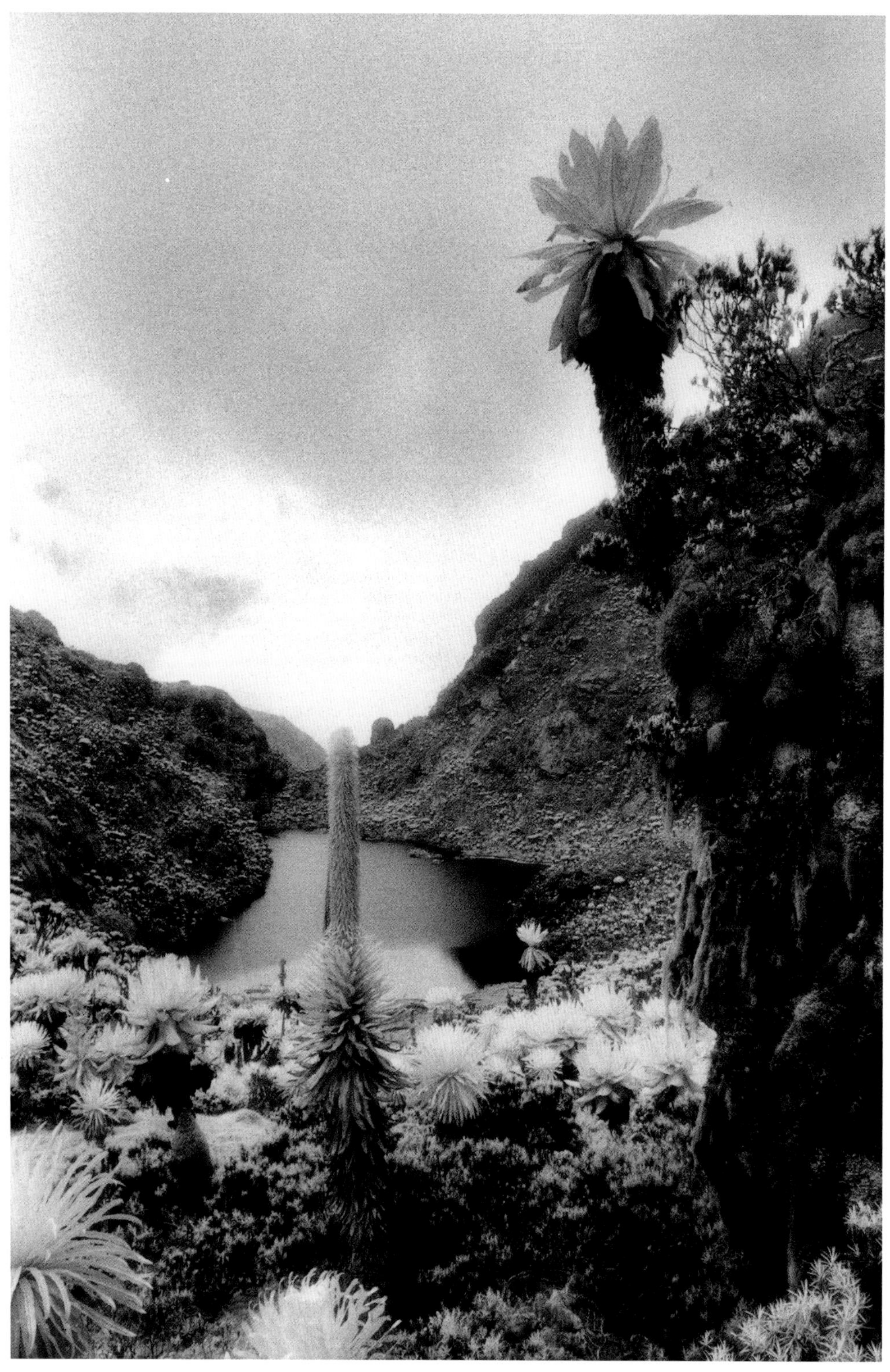

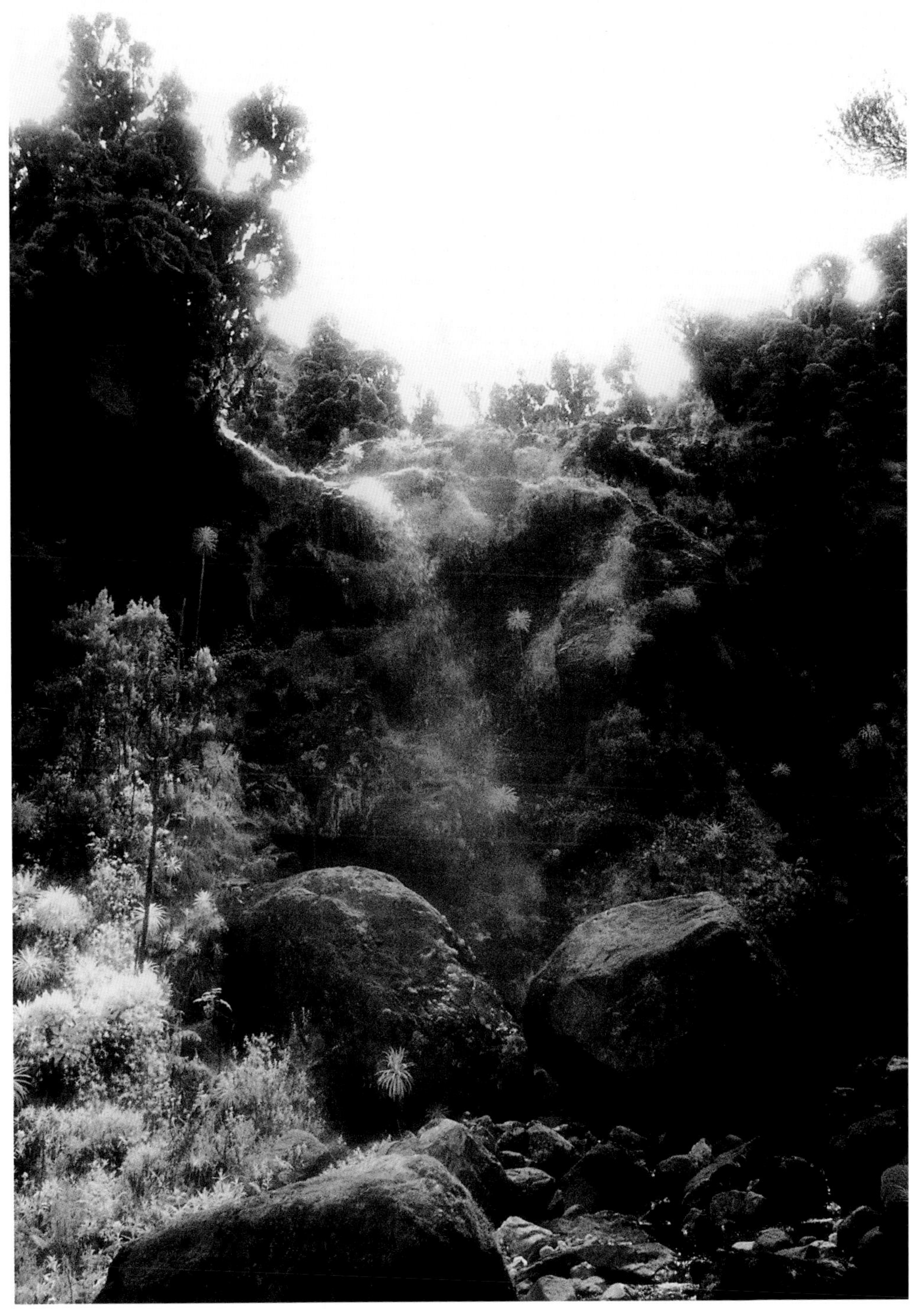

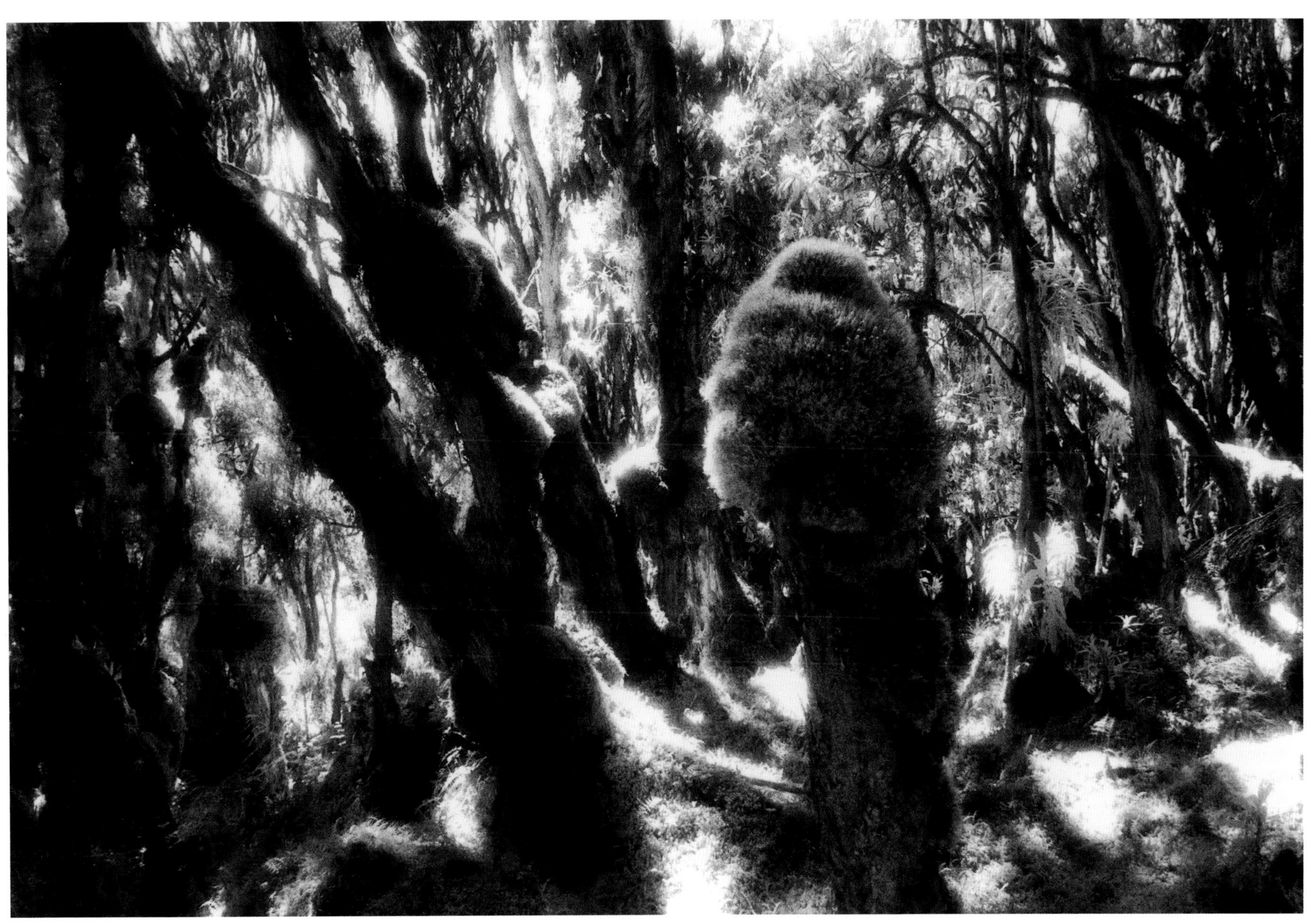

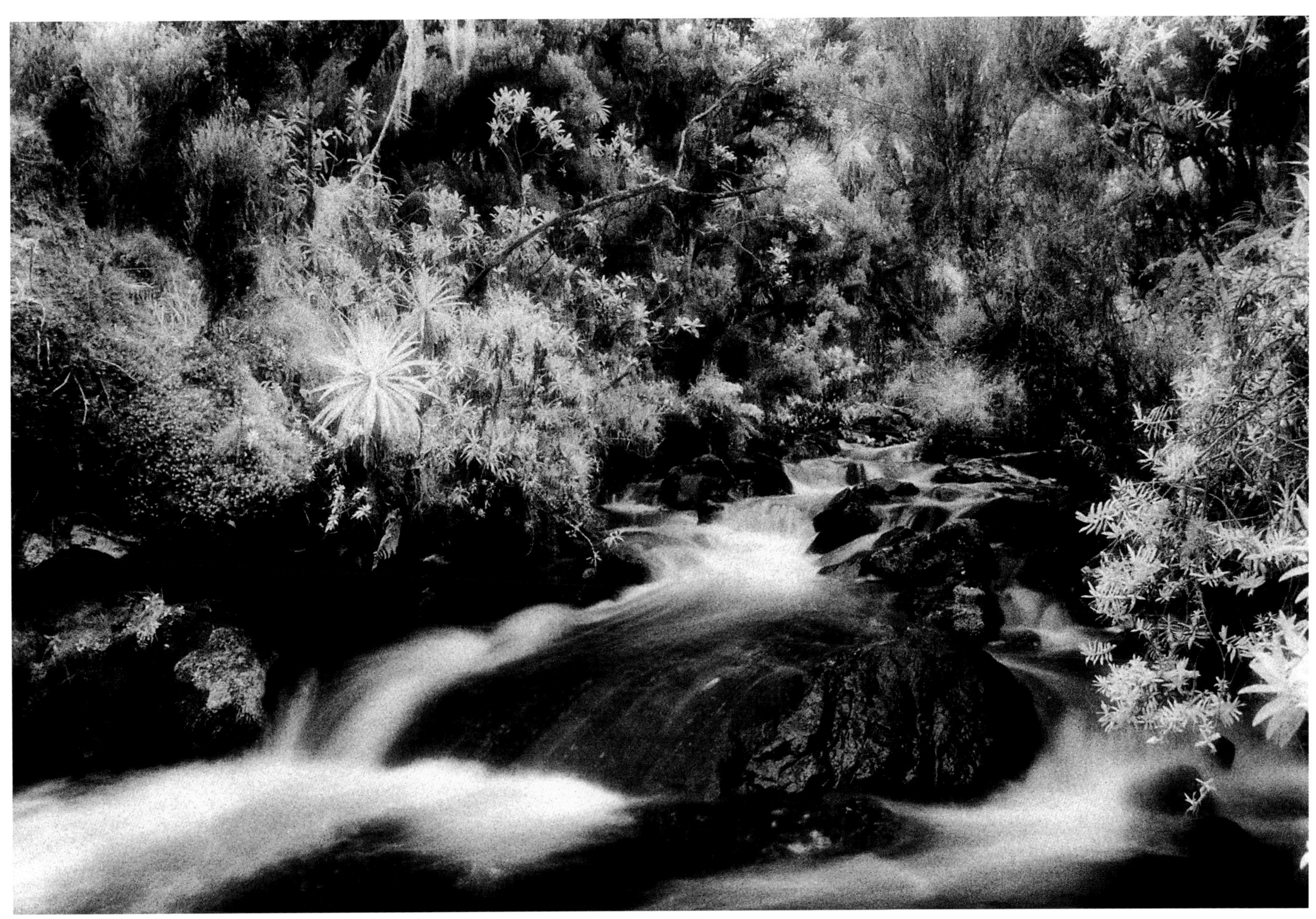

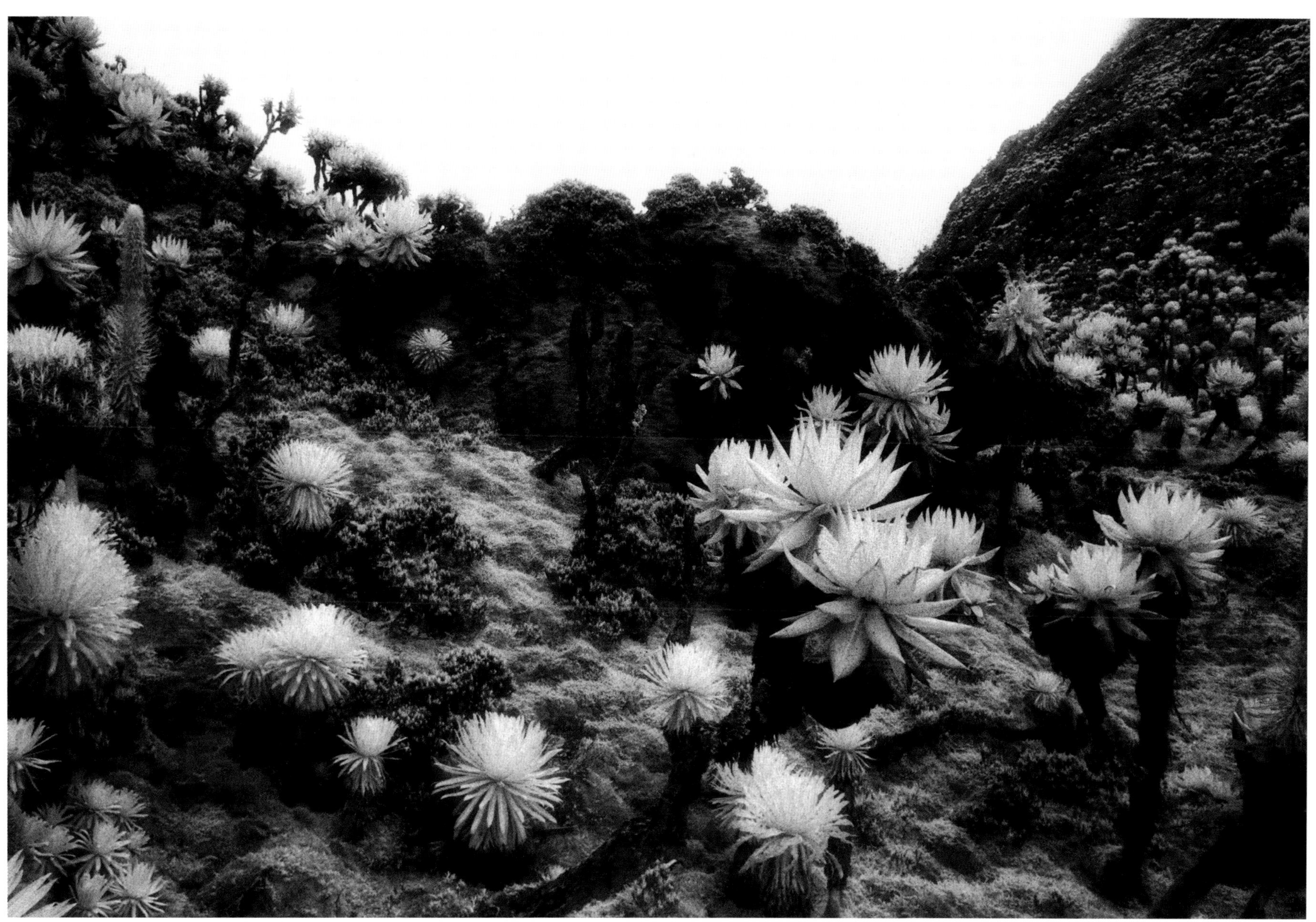

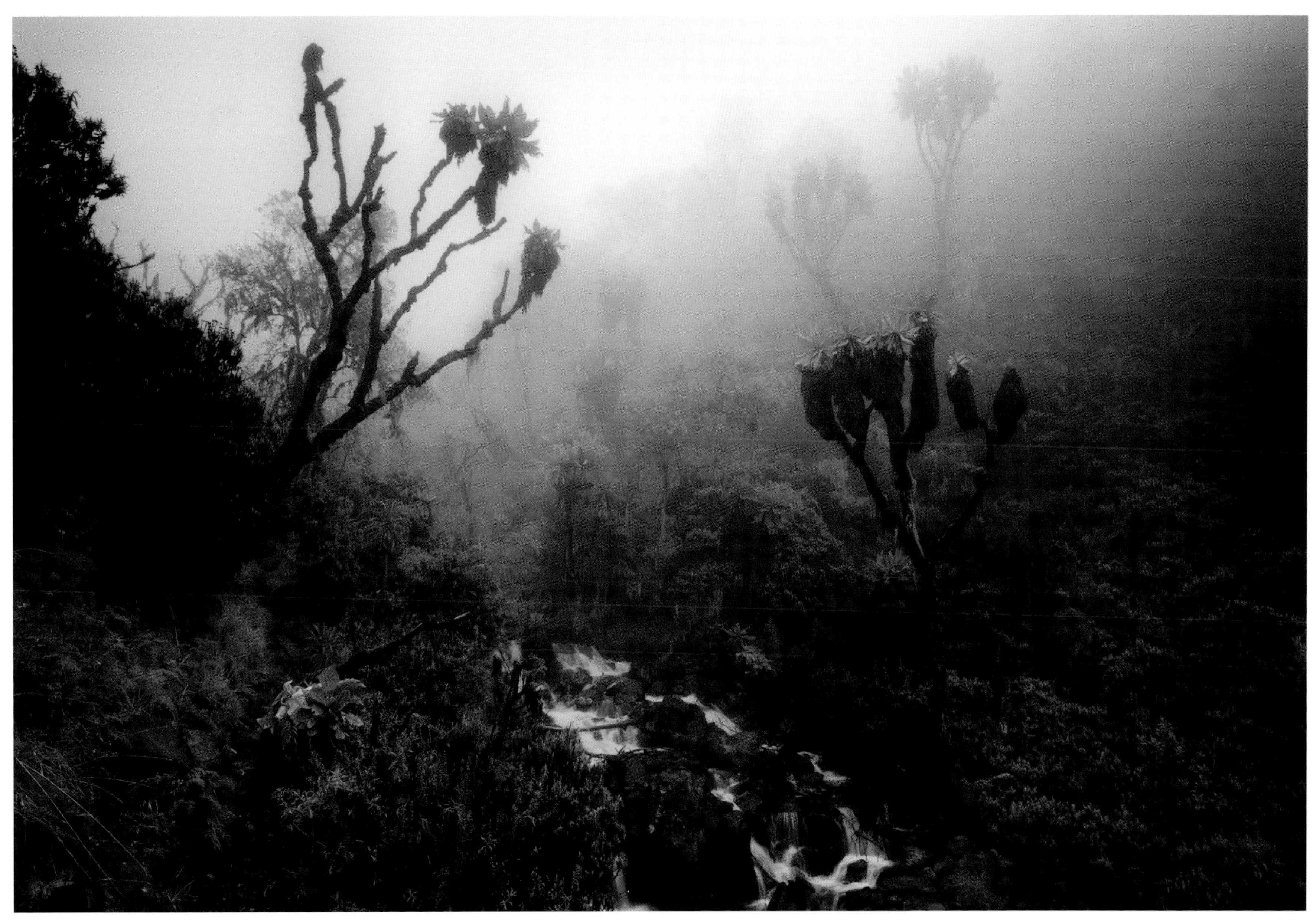

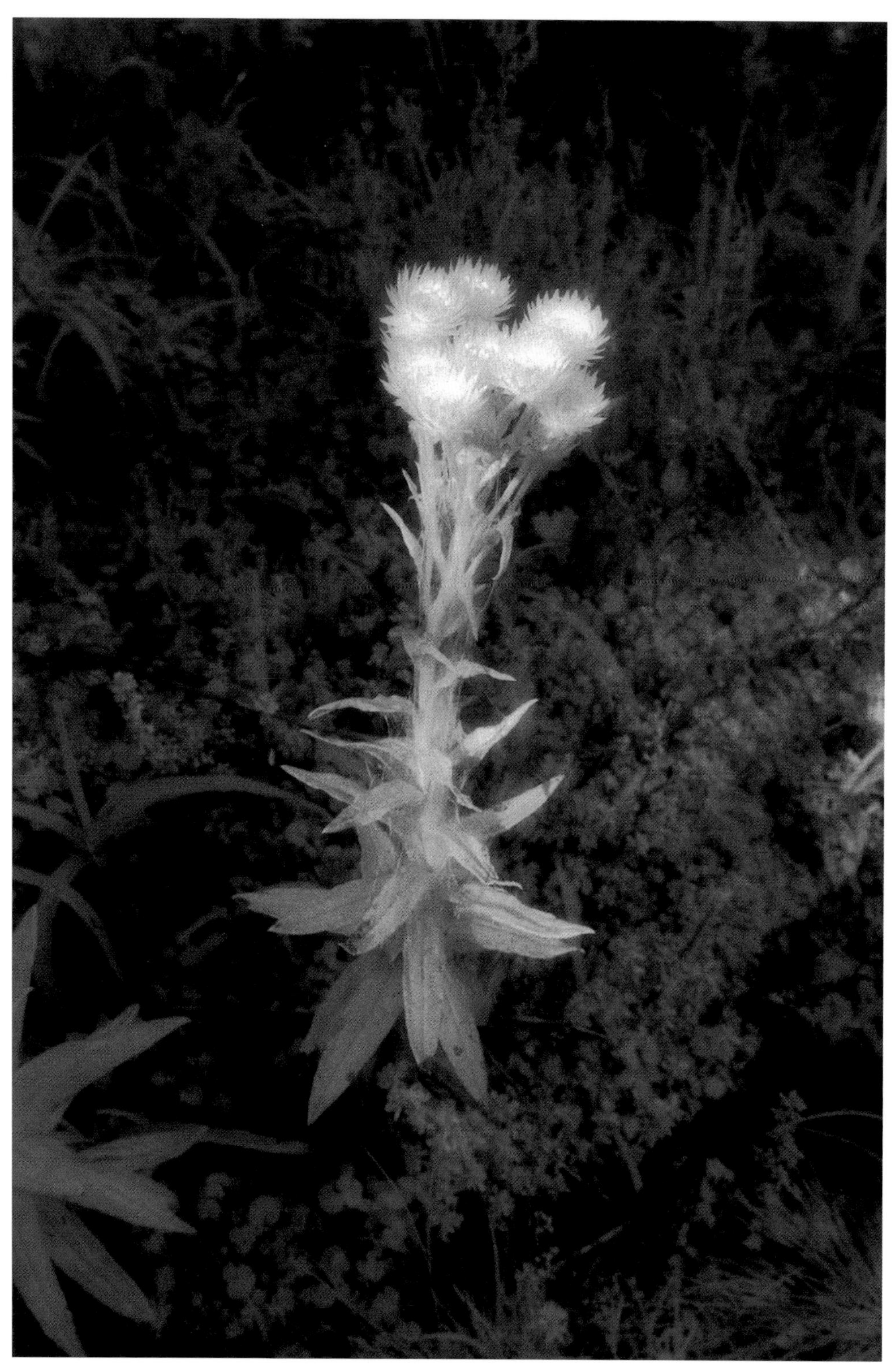

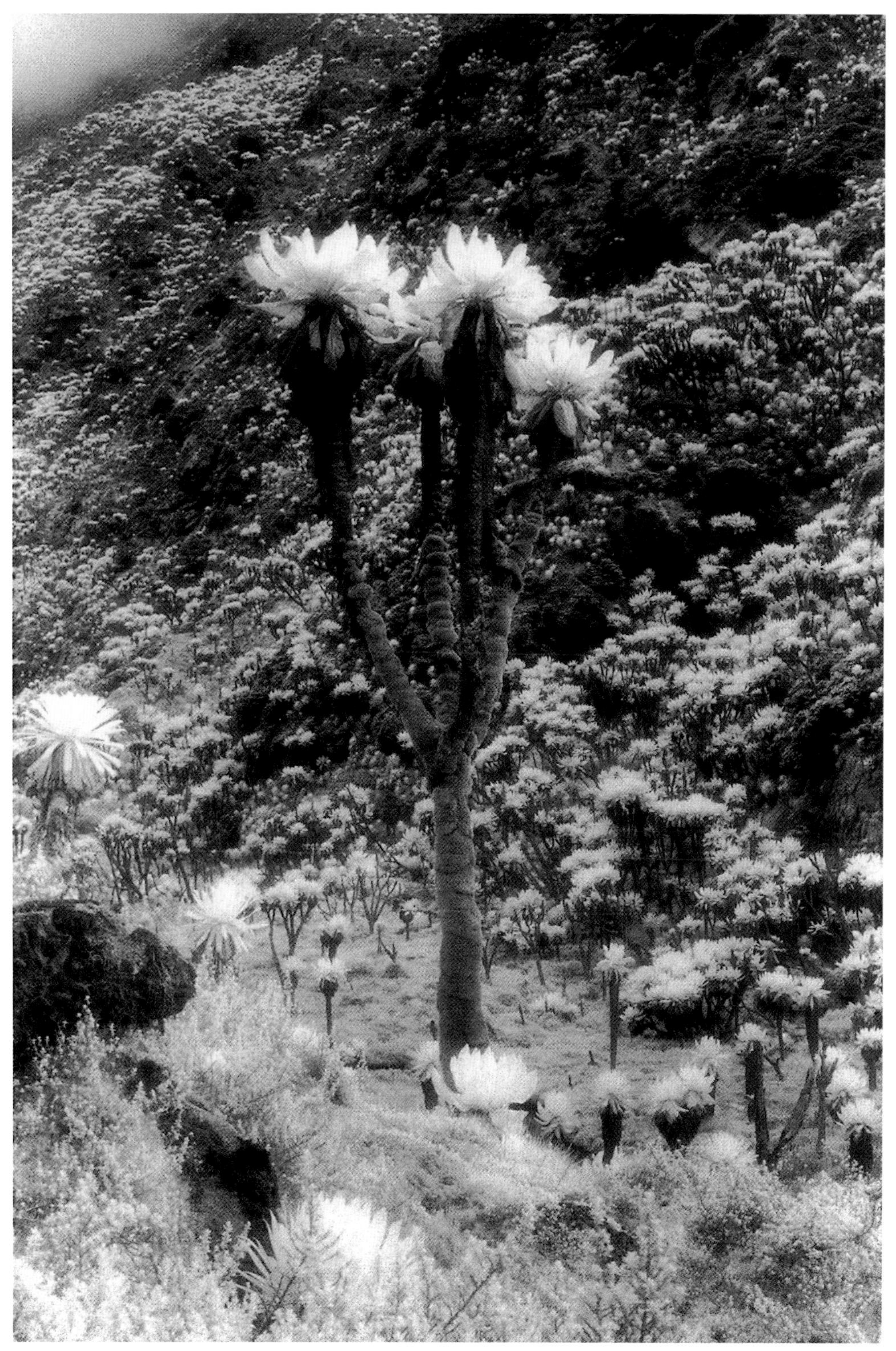

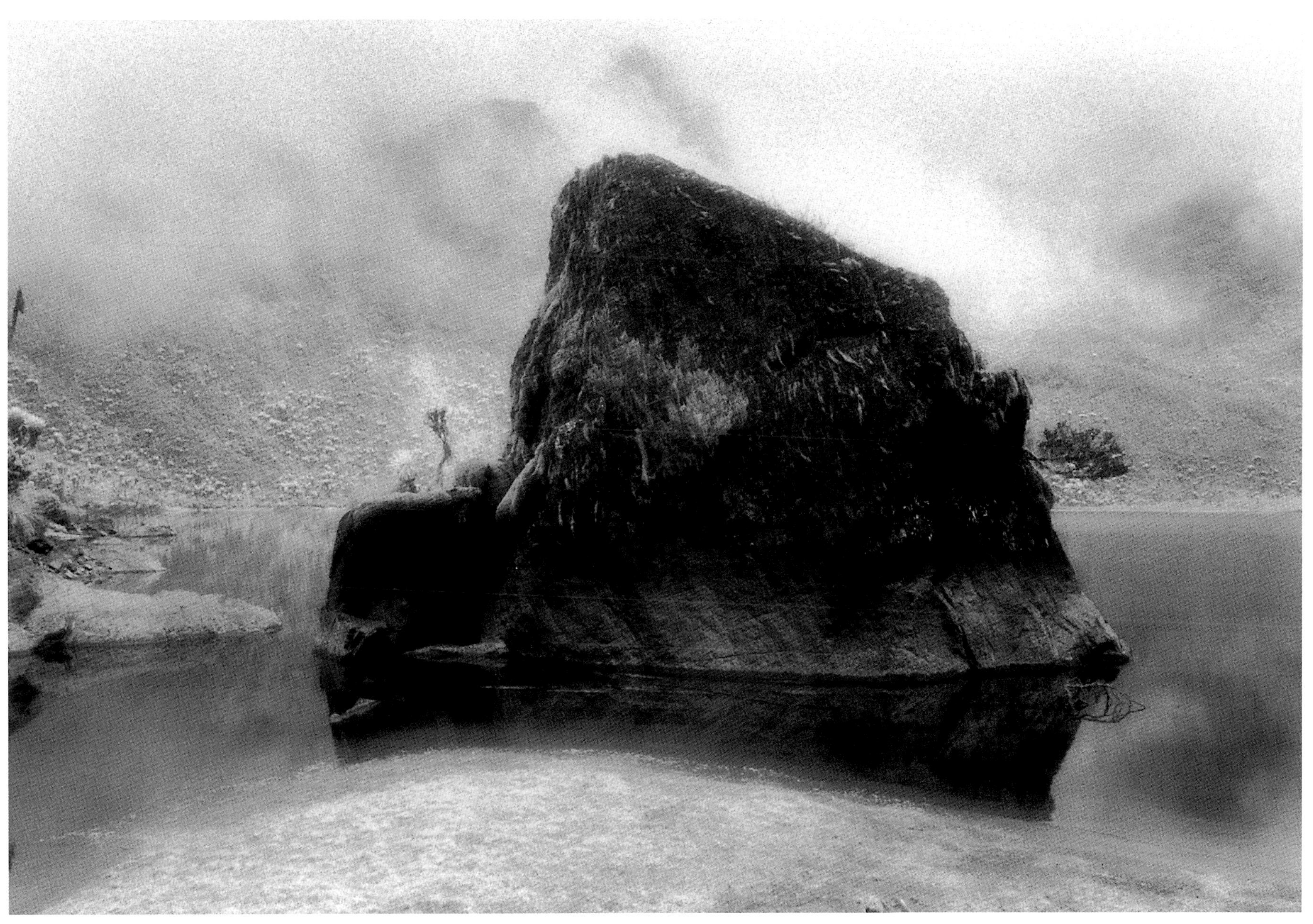

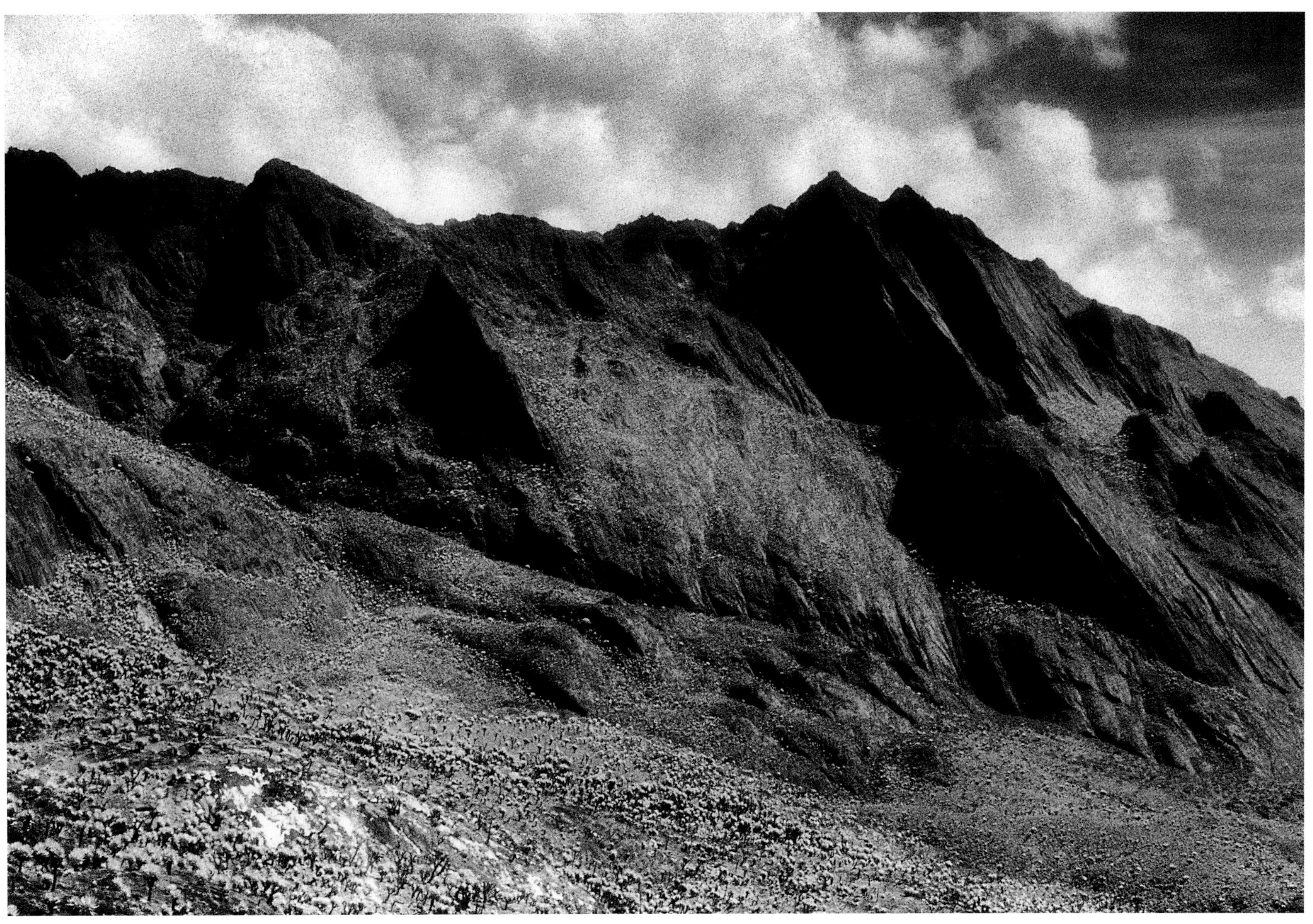

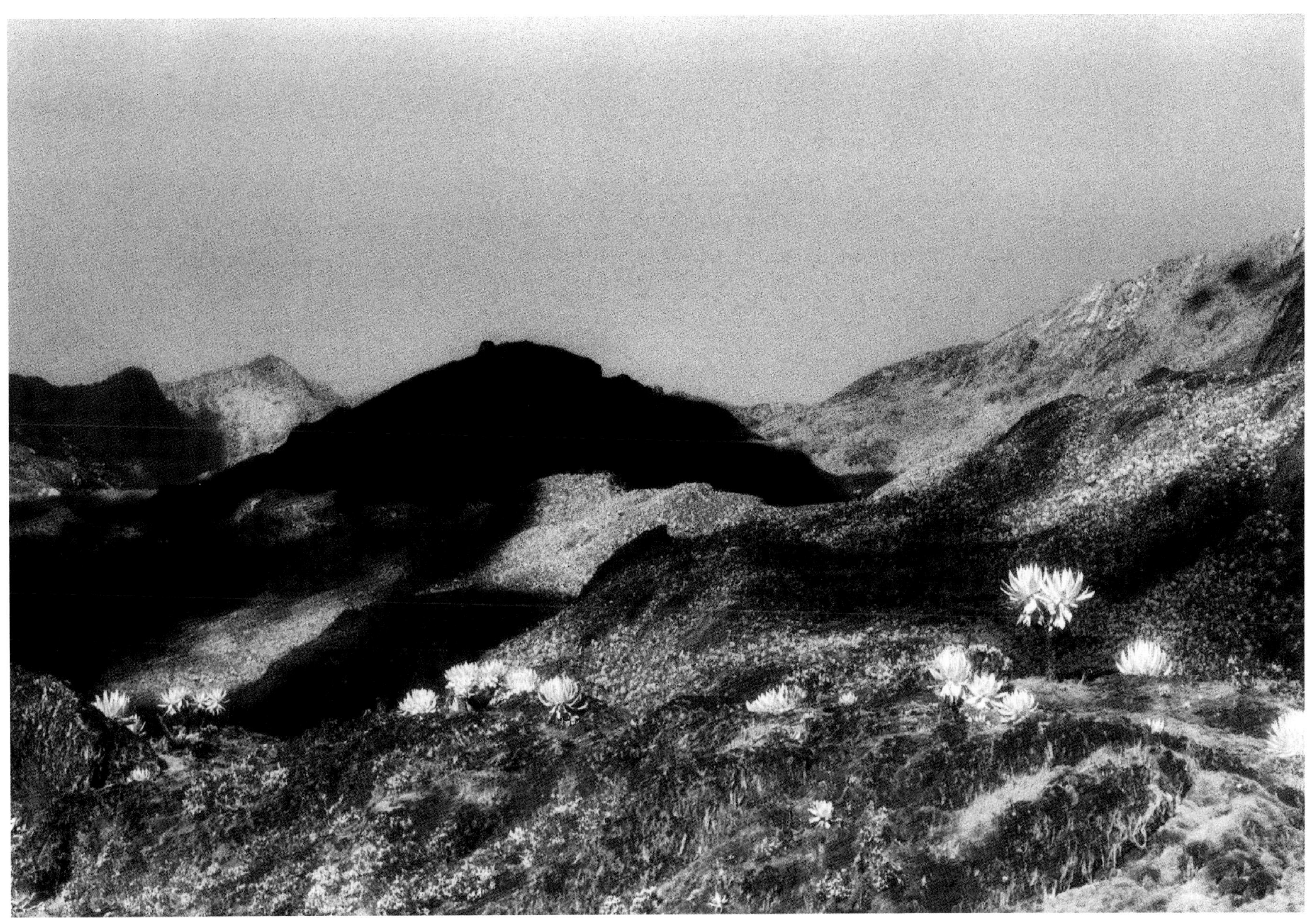

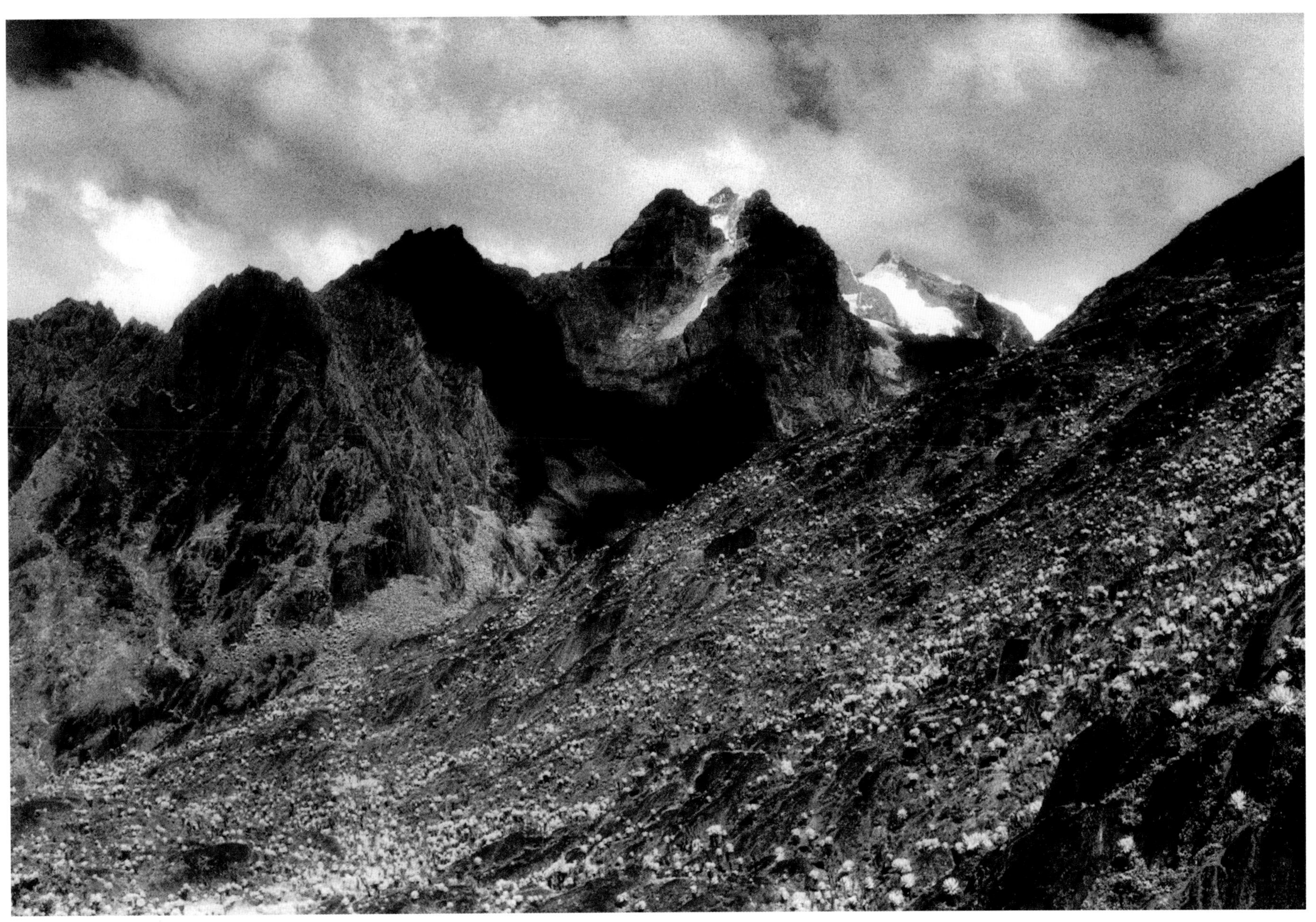

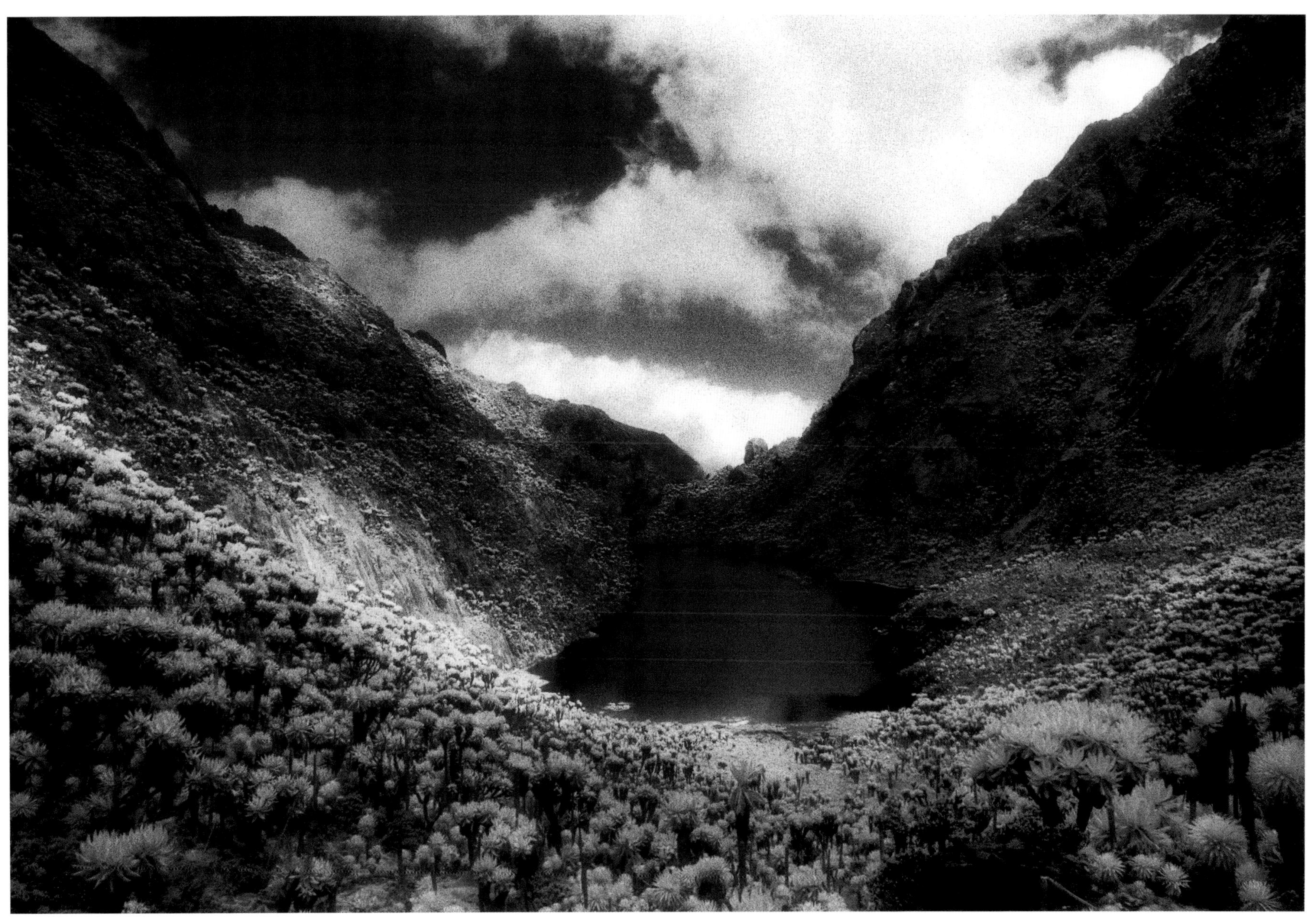

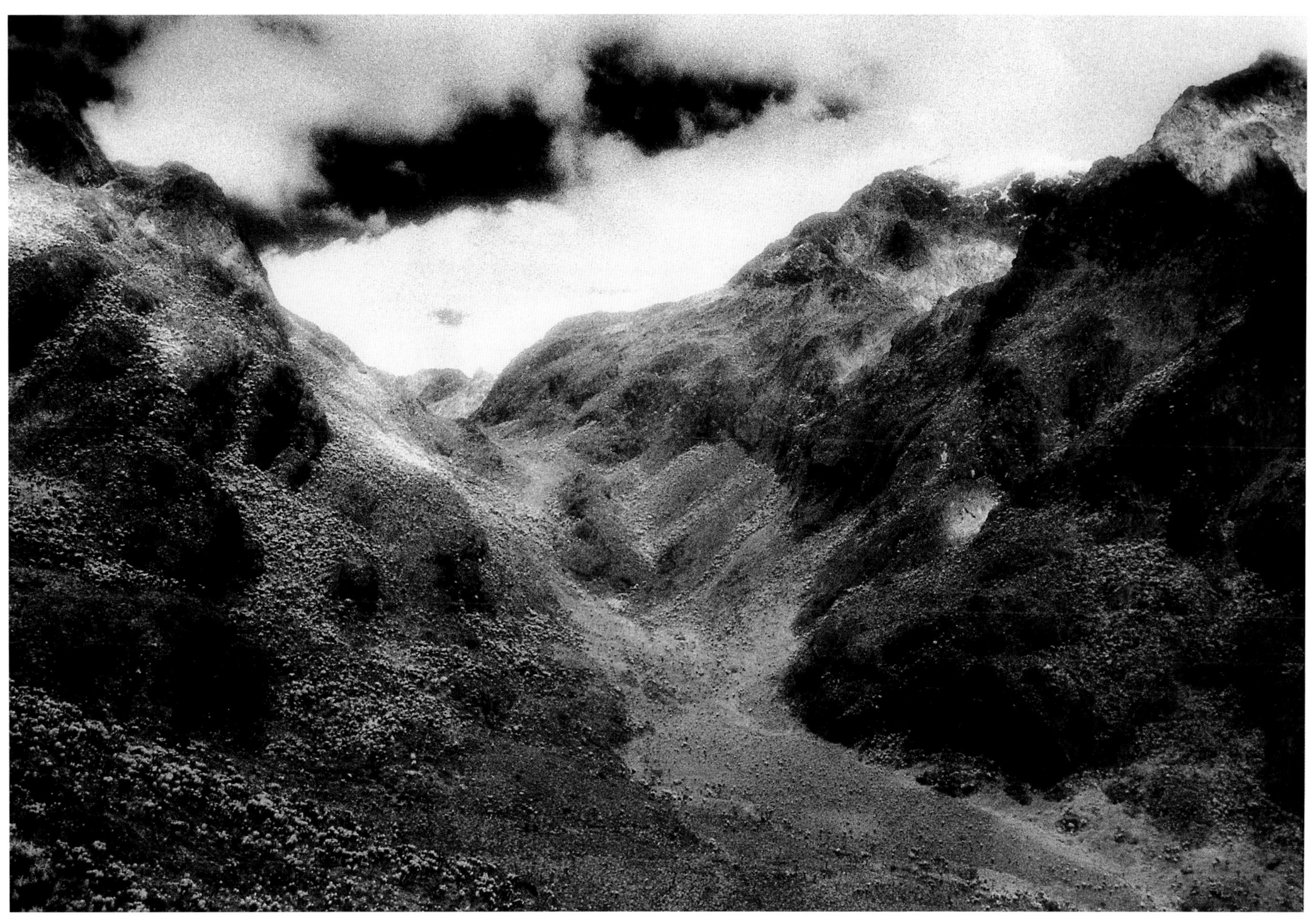

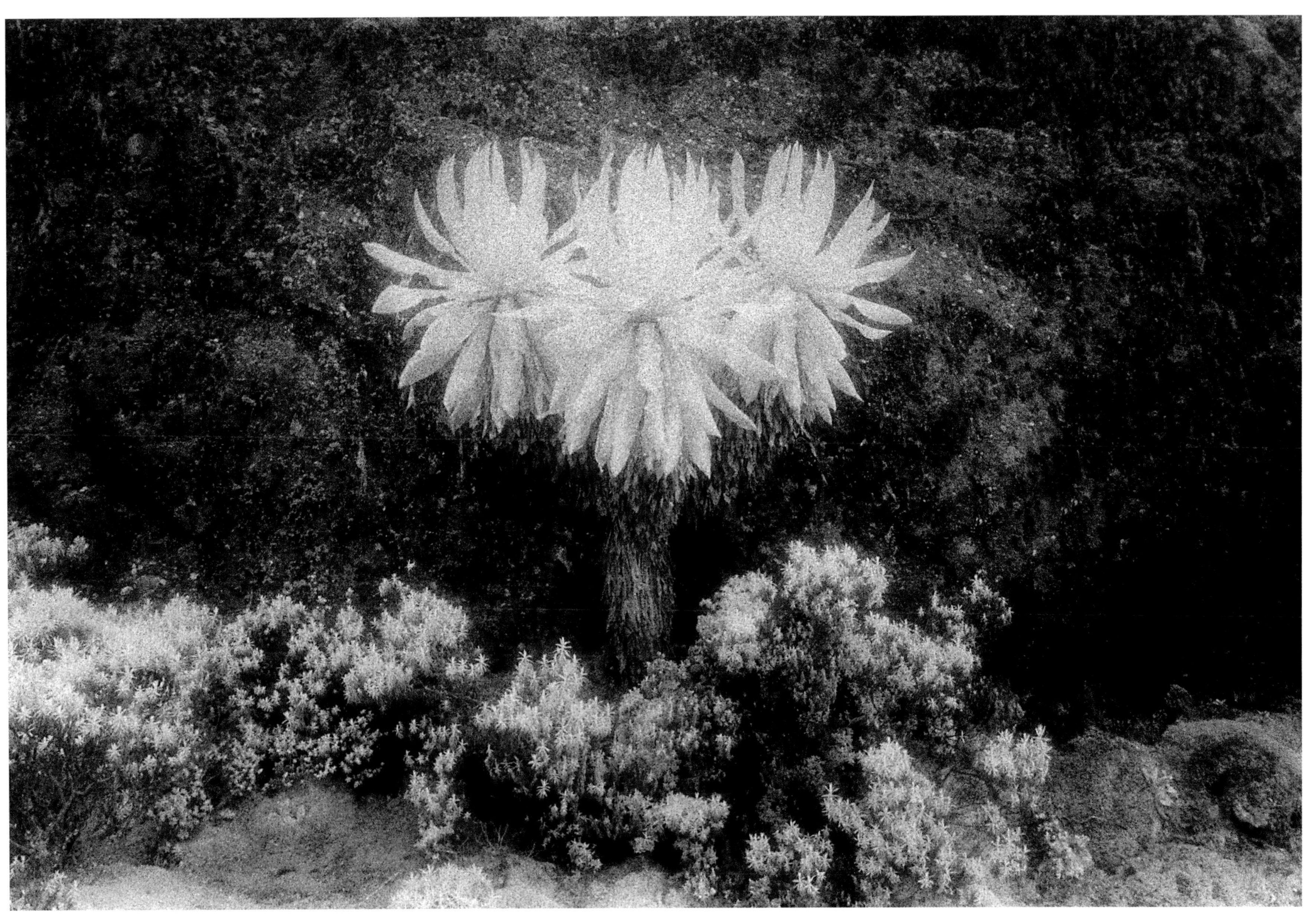